W9-BNQ-746

NARNIA AND BEYOND

THOMAS HOWARD

NARNIA
AND BEYOND

A GUIDE TO THE FICTION OF C. S. LEWIS

With a Foreword by Peter J. Kreeft

IGNATIUS PRESS   SAN FRANCISCO

Previously published under the title
C. S. Lewis: Man of Letters
Ignatius Press, San Francisco
© 1987 by Thomas Howard
All rights reserved

Cover photographs:
Photograph of the lion © Darren Baker
Photograph of the lamp © Jan Tyler

Cover design by John Herreid

© 2006 Ignatius Press, San Francisco
All rights reserved
ISBN 978-1-58617-148-3
ISBN 1-58617-148-8
Library of Congress Control Number 2005909730
Printed in the United States of America ∞

To Mrs. Kilby

For you, dear & noble Lady,
because you
like Mother Dimble & Mrs. Beaver
& Lucy & Tinidril
exhibit to us all,
every day, all day,
what goodness (that is to say, glory)
looks like

CONTENTS

FOREWORD

At last! A book about C. S. Lewis that doesn't sound like a term paper, a book that is a joy to read, a book written with Lewis' own passionate power with words, mercurial magic. At last a book that shows us things we *didn't* see or appreciate in Lewis before, instead of trotting out a recital of the obvious things we did see (unless we were morons).

At last a book that looks *along* Lewis rather than merely *at* him; a book that looks at something far more important than Lewis: his world, which is also our world because it is the real world.

So far the plethora of Lewisiana has illustrated two maxims: that inflation cheapens value and that the more interesting the author, the duller the books about him. To see the first maxim, all you need do is live in America. During inflation, the value of gold soars. We are living through a Lewis inflation, and here is some gold.

For the second maxim, first read Homer, Plato, Saint Augustine, or Kierkegaard, then read any commentary you can find about them. Better yet, first read the most exciting book in the world (the Bible of course), and then read a few dozen of the thousands of astonishingly dull books about it.

Lewis is a magnificent writer, strong and soaring. But with only a few exceptions, books about him have been leaden-footed and platitudinous. Here is the most notable exception so far.

What makes it exceptional is that it accomplishes the two things a good book should aim at, according to the sane, sunny common sense of pre-modern, pre-publish-or-perish literary criticism: "to please and instruct". That is to say, it offers the human spirit its two most essential foods: joy and truth. Lewis does this; that's why he moves us so, and why most books about him don't. Throw them away and read Lewis again. Why eat hamburger when you can eat steak? Why read by reflected moonlight when you can read by direct sunlight? Why look at a photograph when you can look at the real thing?

Why read this book then? Doesn't any book about Lewis merely shed snow on his bell? The shape may be faithful to the bell, but the snow blurs it a bit; and the sound may be the bell's sound, but the snow muffles it a bit. Why not blow away this new snow and hear the naked bell ring out again?

Because this book is not just more snow on the bell. It is an echo chamber, a corridor through which those reverberating bell tones can reach into silent, empty rooms and tombs. It is a witness preaching the ancient and universal Gospel of a glory-filled universe to mousy Modern Man, opening a window onto a world that is not modernity's dungeon but the Great Dance; not *Playboy*'s playpen, but Providence's play, the Cosmic Drama; not the formulas of flatness but the fountain, the hierarchy, the Great Chain of being, packed with peril and drenched in joy: this world is like Aslan—it's not tame, but it's good.

Tom Howard takes the delightful trouble to make this worldview, which is implicit in all Lewis' fiction, explicit in this book. Because he believes, together with "the democracy of the dead", together with all premodern, presecular civilizations, that it is the true world; that nothing is more important than living in the true world; and that one of the most effective ways to waken us out of our little dram world into the enormous, terrifying and wonderful real world is through the imagination of a master storyteller. And who can do this better than the author of *Chance or the Dance*?

I would no more put snow on Howard's bell than he on Lewis'. My prophetic burden is: look with Tom Howard (not at him), and Lewis tells you to look with the world, along the world (not at it). If you do, you will see the ancient stars shining through the modern smog. We are "lost in a haunted wood"; why should we always be staring at the ground? Lift up your eyes, O Jerusalem, and see the "weight of glory".

What an unfashionable task for a book today. Hopelessly naïve, of course. Simple-mindedness, wish-fulfillments, desperate dreams. Science has conclusively demonstrated that ... modern scholarship is unanimous that ... the consensus of the most enlightened opinion assures us that ...

Oh, shut up, Screwtape! Go on, reader, I dare you. Take another look.

— *Peter J. Kreeft*

PREFACE

C. S. Lewis' *Chronicles of Narnia* began appearing in the United States in the early 1950s. They made a stir then; but presently the stir became an insistent sound, which itself became eventually a roar, so to speak. By the time of this writing, two, or perhaps three, generations of children have been regaled by these "fairy tales" (as Lewis called them). And indeed they are fairy tales, in the best tradition of that genre. Everything is here: spells; talking animals; fauns; centaurs; unicorns (or at least *a* unicorn); witches; dryads; heroes; and, best of all, a lion who turns out to be the Son of the Emperor Beyond the Sea.

There is an irony in all of this, however. The thing is, what we find extolled in the Chronicles are such odd qualities as purity, humility, fidelity, valor, courtesy, domesticity, simplicity, and *holiness*, forsooth. This is all very well, but the point is that virtually every one of these qualities has long since been buried and forgotten in the avalanche which has swept over Western civilization in the last fifty years. The boulders and rubble in this avalanche have such names as "self-authentication", "self-actualization", "self-assertion", and "self-promotion", and with all of this comes a certain harshness, callousness, cynicism, and a thing which calls itself liberation, which is as old as mankind itself, namely the indulgence in ribald forms of public sexual license which would make Babylon itself blush.

But this is to strike an unhappy note. The Chronicles are full of pure joy. Glorious, hilarious, rhapsodic joy. To be sure, there is sorrow, and terror and wistfulness and horrible evil. But Lewis is like Dante: he knew that Joy is a higher and deeper word than sorrow. He knew that Joy is the Last Word. *The Chronicles of Narnia* are a "comedy" in the old sense of that word. It does not mean lots of laughs. Rather, it refers to a tale that ends in marriage, whatever ordeals may have gone before. Readers already versed in the Chronicles may object here that there is no marriage in Narnia. No. Not as such, of course. But that great rush at the end, when Jewel the Unicorn leads them all in a great race "farther up and farther in", is akin to the glorious consummation of all things which we find in Dante, and, before that, in Christian revelation itself. It is the ingathering of all of God's people into his kingdom, the way a bride is brought into the household of her lord or, in this case, the way all of the good creatures in Narnia are swept up into Aslan's country.

The interest in Narnia seems, suddenly, to have exploded in our decade. This may be due, in part, to the worldwide fascination with Tolkien's saga. And it makes sense: Lewis and Tolkien wrote about, and loved, the same world, and they read their manuscripts to each other over the years when they were working on them. We can only hope that the lovely, and even salvific, effects of their tales may keep alive in those who love these stories, something of the sheer goodness that obtains in Middle Earth and in Narnia.

— *Thomas Howard*
November 2005

CHAPTER ONE

The Peal of a
Thousand Bells

In the early days of World War II, an odd book appeared in England and America. It seemed to be a collection of letters from an old devil to a younger one, telling him how to handle a man who had been assigned to him as his special demonic responsibility.

The book was odd for a number of reasons. For a start, one does not run across infernal letters every day. But then this was not a book on the occult, nor demonism, nor satanism, nor any other sort of arcana. Moreover, it was odd in that, in the darkest days that the West had known for many a century, it caught the attention of Christendom, not by commenting on the dread and apocalyptic political situation we found ourselves in just then, but rather on a much older, more widespread, and infinitely more alarming situation that the race has lived with for aeons. And again, it was odd in that, right in the middle of the twentieth century, after decades of assiduous effort on the part of the modern Church in the West to "de-supernaturalize" the ancient Faith under the gun of German romanticism, higher criticism, Darwinism, Freudianism, and so forth (this effort was called "modernism")—just when this effort had swept all before it in Protestantism at least—there appeared this book which assumed, blithely and unapologetically, that the *Devil* is real, for heaven's sake. Here was Christian theology, anxiously plucking at the coattails of the Western world, assuring everyone that we don't for a moment insist that anyone believe in any nonsense about miracles and God-in-the-flesh, and parthenogenesis and so forth, much less *Satan*, and along comes a book, not by a white-sock stump-preacher from the boondocks, but by a vastly civilized and luminously intelligent don who obviously *believed* this awkward stuff.

The book, of course, was *The Screwtape Letters*, and the don was Clive Staples Lewis.

Who was he? Well, he was a Christian, for a start, of the Anglican variety. But no group in Christendom can claim him as its special spokesman. He was most emphatically a "mere" Christian, meaning by that, not a watered-down Christian, but a Christian who saw himself as standing in the mainstream of traditional orthodoxy, as that has been taught and held universally for two thousand years (*quod ubique, quod semper, quod ab omnibus creditum est*—what has everywhere, always, and by everyone been believed: the old Vincentian Canon would apply to him quite well). He took the Bible seriously, but the evangelicals couldn't claim him; and he was unselfconsciously a sacramentalist, but the Anglo-Catholics couldn't claim him. He was Anglican, but Methodists and Roman Catholics and Baptists read him and applauded. He saw as his particular apostolate the task of speaking as plainly as he knew how, in as many ways as he knew how, of the Gospel.

Who was this ruddy apologist with the baggy tweeds, booming voice, bald head, horn-rimmed specs, and sensitive nostrils? The British were becoming aware of him by the time *The Screwtape Letters* appeared in 1942; his voice was coming to them frequently over the BBC in a series of "Broadcast Talks" defending Christian orthodoxy. Anyone who has ever heard that voice pursuing its lucid and relentless way through an argument, or who has read *Mere Christianity* (the title given to the published collection of three of his series of BBC talks) knows something of the sheer force and magnificence of Lewis in argument. There is nothing snide, nothing petty, nothing *ad hominem*, disingenuous, or irrelevant. All is magnanimity, clarity, and craftsmanship. Lewis knew backward and forward the *art* of argument—of rhetoric, actually, in its Renaissance meaning, designating the whole enterprise of opening up and articulating and working through a given line of thought.

He had been taught this by a tutor whom he called "The Great Knock". This man, whose name was Kirkpatrick, had taken Lewis as a private pupil in 1914, after Lewis' schooldays, which had been mostly unhappy, not because Lewis was a dull student (he wasn't) but because he hated English public school life with its hearty and vulgar *bonhomie*, its enforced games, and the general caddishness of the "bloods".

The Great Knock was an atheist, and Lewis went up to Oxford in 1917, having had every vestige of religion scoured from his being. The desultory Anglicanism of his background had flagged during his schooldays, and now it was gone indeed. Like most young atheists, Lewis felt brisk and free. God's not in his heaven, all may not be right with the world (Lewis in fact left Oxford for a year or two for the trenches of France, where he was wounded), but at least I am in control.

Unhappily for Lewis' spanking-new atheism, God, who was not supposed to be there, began to crowd in on him during the next decade. To his chagrin he discovered that the people he admired and liked the most at Oxford were turning out, one after the other, to be *Christians*. A tiresome business. It's all very well for old ladies at Evensong, and for Baptist evangelists; but Oxonians? God was the last thing Lewis felt like encountering, but he does not appear to have been given much choice in the matter (always affirming, of course, the mystery of free will). He tells the story of his reluctant conversion in his spiritual autobiography, *Surprised by Joy*. Finally, as he puts it, ". . . the fox was in the open". No more cover. The chase was on, the Hound in full cry. And he was caught. In 1929 he knelt in his rooms at Magdalen College, the unhappiest man in England that night, and admitted that "God is God." It was a conversion to theism. Two years later, riding in the sidecar of his brother Warnie's motorcycle en route to Whipsnade Zoo, he crossed the line into Christian faith. He puts it this way: "When we set out I did not believe that Jesus Christ is the Son of God, and when we reached the zoo I did."

This makes it sound capricious and subjective in the extreme, as though one chases religious impressions like foxfires in a swamp. To have this notion dispelled, one may read *Surprised by Joy*. Lewis' conversion was the least "religious" conversion imaginable, if by religious we mean rhapsodic, or emotional, or impressionistic. It was almost entirely an intellectual conversion, as far as Lewis understood it at the time. His *mind* was commandeered by God: he became convinced of the philosophically untenable nature of atheism, then of agnosticism; then the Christian claims began to seem not so out of the question, and so forth.

The rest of the story is mainly the story of books. Lewis' life was humdrum, judged by the sensationalism dinned at us so shrilly by TV and popular journalism. He never traveled. His holidays tended to be "walking holidays", that favorite pastime of Oxford dons, when they take a map and a stick, put on old shoes, and set out for the Cotswolds, Westmoreland, or the West Highlands. He moved in no chic literary/artistic circles like Evelyn Waugh's or Virginia Woolf's. He liked monotony—he sought it—since monotony (not to be confused with ennui) allows one the luxury of getting on with one's work with some sort of rhythm and regularity and tranquillity.

There were no major "events" in Lewis' life. His career went along slowly. Oxford University never honored him with a professorship, even though he was a formidable scholar and a popular lecturer. Many observers have attributed this to a certain pique on the part of the university over Lewis' unabashed Christian witness and his insistence on writing book after book "not in his field"—space fantasies, and Christian apologetics, and children's books forsooth. It was all so unbecoming.

In the end, it was the "other" university that honored him. In 1955, Cambridge offered him the Professorship of Mediaeval and Renaissance Literature at its Magdalene (spelled with an *e*) College, and he accepted. The only *event* in his life was his marriage to Joy Davidman in 1956. She was a victim of cancer, and they had what they thought was a deathbed marriage ceremony. But she was granted a remission (Lewis saw it as a healing miracle), and he experienced with her in later middle life all the intense romantic joy that had passed him by in his youth. The ravaging and profound grief at her death in 1960 is recorded in his book *A Grief Observed*, which appeared in 1961 under the pseudonym of N. W. Clerk, but which immediately had all readers familiar with Lewis' style scrutinizing every line narrowly under the strong suspicion that this was none other than Lewis himself. He died on November 22, 1963, the day John F. Kennedy was shot.

Not a terribly exciting life. It would be hard to make a big box-office film out of it. But one wonders whether, five thousand years from now when the archaeologists are sifting through the dust of our epoch, they won't end up with Lewis' name among a very few others as one who had a long-lasting effect on the race.

One might also venture to guess that it will be on the basis of his works of imagination as much as on his essays and apologetics that Lewis' lasting reputation will rest.

One way of putting what Lewis saw as his literary task would be to say that he wanted to lead his readers to a window, looking out from the dark and stuffy room of modernity, and to burst open the shutters and point us all to an enormous vista stretching away from the room in which we are shut. He despaired of finding any furniture, pictures, or objects *in* that small room that would suggest what he wanted to say to us; we must come to the window and look *out*.

It sounds odd to speak of modernity as a dark and stuffy room. Our common, blithe supposition is that the last century or two have witnessed our escape from the dark and stuffy room of tradition, and that the whole point of everything since the Enlightenment is, surely, that light has finally been let in, or better still, that we have at last come out into the light. It is the light of emancipation on all fronts. We have come into our real patrimony as human beings: alone in the cosmos, autonomous, self-defining at last. The ancients toiled along, fondly supposing that the gods were there and that men were accountable for their actions to this high tribunal. They thought that there was angelic and demonic traffic hurrying up and down the universe, and that there were bright celestial entities to be adored, and dark infernal entities to be dreaded. They thought that Goodness and Evil were huge fixities; the one was to be sought and the other eschewed, the end of the one being bliss and of the other damnation. They surrounded human behavior with all sorts of taboos, and cluttered things up with sacrifices since (they thought) if they did not they would be in trouble. You couldn't do this and you couldn't do that, not because it was inappropriate but because it was sin.

We now have the tools at our disposal to come at the plain truth of things: the analyst's couch, the test tube, the questionnaire, the computer. These will deliver us, where the aspergillum, the thurible, the Gospel book, and the crucifix failed. It will take a long time, of course, to clear the space, but we are at last beginning, and soon can get down to building the real edifice, the temple of Man.

So runs the contemporary mythology.

Lewis struggled to find a way of speaking to an epoch with which he shared virtually no suppositions at all. He called himself an "Old Western Man", meaning thereby that he held the view of things generally held in Judaeo-Graeco-Christian tradition. He witnessed with dread, even with sickness of soul, the program of modernity and tried to find a way to lodge in the modern imagination some reminder of an alternative vision.

I may illustrate this problem by referring to my own experience of teaching prep school and college students. I have sometimes given a class the following list of words: majesty, magnanimity, valor, courtesy, grace, chastity, virginity, nobility, splendor, ceremony, taboo, mystery, purity. The reaction is quite predictible: a total blank, embarrassed snickers, or incredulity. The entire list of words lands in their laps like a heap of dead basalt meteorites lately arrived from some other realm. They don't know what to do with them. They have never encountered them. The words are entirely foreign to the whole set of assumptions that has been written (or I should say televised) into these students' imaginations for the whole of their lives. Majesty? The man must be mad. Valor? What's that? Courtesy? What a bore. Virginity? Ho-ho—there's one for you! Chuckle, chuckle.

After I have gotten my reaction I point out to them that this awful list of words names an array of qualities that any Jew, any pagan, and any Christian, up until quite recently in history, would have not only understood, but would have extolled as being close to the center of things. Their vision of reality presented them with a picture in which these things appeared as not only natural, but blissful.

Lewis understood the daunting improbability of awakening the stultified modern imagination to ancient and eternal blisses and realities. He understood the task, and he undertook it by means of the oldest method there is. He began to tell stories (sometimes you can smuggle something in as fiction that you can't force on people in a debate). His best-known tales are his *Chronicles of Narnia*. After them would come his space fiction—or rather his "Deep Heaven" fiction: space is one of the modern ideas that he thought inadequate to the reality.

On one accounting Lewis' stories are terribly wrongheaded. They are full of pernicious ideas that ought to be eliminated, if we pay attention to the committees that sit somewhere deep in governmental bureaus and tell us what we may do with our souls and our children's souls. There is a king, for example. This is bad, because it will lodge in our children's imaginations a notion that is incompatible with the egalitarian frame of mind we work so assiduously to inculcate in them. Here we are, in their early, impressionable years, regaling them with all these scenes of majesty in Narnia. And the worst of it is that the king is *good*. It might do to have a bad king since it would dramatize the very thing we want to suggest—that absolute authority is by nature tyrannical.

And there is at work in Lewis' worlds a moral order, fixed, serene, absolute, and blissful. We do not like the smell of this. We prefer the imagery of endless quest, and of innovation, and of self-authentication, in which heroes seek but do not find, and in seeking forge their own moral selves on the anvil of passion. For us, the imagery of a fixed moral order is suffocating. It keeps humanity chained in perpetual childhood, groveling before taboos and totems, always trying to live up to some scheme devised by a maleficent deity who knows nothing of what it means to be human. We want Prometheus. It is his defiance of the gods that we find so compelling and suggestive.

But in Lewis' world (indeed in all worlds and moral schemes until our own), we find that the fixed order that presides so serenely and absolutely over the lives and acts of the creatures in that world, not only does not cramp the freedom and selfhood of those creatures, it is synonymous with it. All the creatures find their true identity and liberty in a hierarchical scale in which they have responsibilities of service running in both directions, up and down. The duty they owe to creatures above them is one of fealty, or of respect, and perhaps even of awe. The duty they owe to those below is the duty of magnanimity. Either way it is a matter of service and obedience: the proper service offered in courtesy to the creature in question.

An example from Lewis' worlds may illustrate this. In *Perelandra* the hero, Ransom, encounters celestial beings of inexpressible majesty called *eldila* (perhaps akin to angels in our own story). The *eldila* charged with the oversight of any given planet are called *Oyeresu* (the plural of *Oyarsa*). Ransom meets two of these, Perelandra and Malacandra, better known to us by their Roman names, Venus and Mars. They are so terrible in their splendor that they have difficulty in finding forms under which Ransom can even bear to encounter them. Ransom, of course, assumes that all possible esteem is due these great deities, and he is correct. But lo and behold, when the man and woman who are king and queen of Perelandra (the planet has the same name as its *Oyarsa*) appear, the two *eldila* do obeisance to *them*. There is no struggle for equal time, no eyeball-to-eyeball confrontation, no quarrel over precedence, no ad hoc committee of the whole to determine equal authority for the whole caucus. No. There is rather the solemn hierarchic dance of majesty encountering majesty, and of sovereignty joyously given and received. The man and woman are to the planet Perelandra what the unfallen Adam and Eve are to Earth. For their part, they offer courtesy to the two *eldila* in obedience to some cosmic protocol; but just as obediently they receive the obeisance of those *eldila* because it is their appointed burden and glory to do so.

Another example of this: in Narnia we find the land populated by dwarfs, fauns, dryads, centaurs, giants, and Talking Beasts. It is their land. They are its rightful denizens. But it turns out that neither the land nor these denizens can be fully free and fully themselves unless there are sons of Adam and daughters of Eve (that is to say, humans) on the Four Thrones in the palace of Cair Paravel.

The point here is not to urge monarchy over democracy but to recognize that Lewis has shown us a world in which a hierarchical order is seen in terms of courtesy, magnanimity, and obedience, and is the guarantor of everyone's liberty. He was not speaking of politics when he wrote about Narnia, so much as picturing a world in which obedience and liberty were synonymous. But you can't come at this idea via a democratic imagery, so Lewis gave that world the ancient ordering of hierarchy. Any Christian is familiar with this moral paradox and affirms it, since he worships a God whose service is perfect freedom. To the egalitarian point of view it is nonsense, but there it is at the center of things, and in Narnia we find it played out in the colorful imagery of animals, fauns, and human beings.

Lewis would be able to point, in this connection, to an oddity in the history of human imagination that has escaped our notice lately, but that supports his vision. It is this: that the ages which assumed and acknowledged a hierarchical order have produced the most splendid works of imagination. It is when the gods are enthroned in their heavens that you find tall heroes and noble heroines peopling the tales. Greek tragedy, Nordic saga, Shakespearean tragedy, and thirteenth-century figures of the Virgin crowned with gold all embody the paradox. It is when you have set humanity free from the fixed order that you start getting Willie Loman, and Andy Warhol's antiheroes. It is anomalous that Achilles, Hector, Beowulf, Siegfried, Arthur, and Macbeth are such magnificent figures—to say nothing of Antigone, Penelope, Deborah, and Cleopatra. They all had the gods peering over their shoulders. They ought to have been crawling and sniveling.

This notion of moral fixity seems repressive to moderns. What we need, we say, for our authentic freedom, is spontaneity, functionalism, and self-determination. But Lewis would have pointed us to the picture of things that all poets, prophets, sages, and saints have lauded, namely that, paradoxically, we grow into our real selfhood and liberty by learning the steps in the Dance. The Dance is there. It is already choreographed. The music is playing. All creatures— all stars, all archangels, all lions and eagles and oak trees and seas and clams and grasshoppers—are dancing. The great thing is to learn the steps appointed for you and to move into your place.

The idea is at work in Lewis' novel *That Hideous Strength*. The whole drama here is of a young man and woman— man and wife they are—who find themselves bundled all cock-a-hoop into *Charity*, when that is not at all what they wanted. What they wanted was self-determination (which was what they had, and they were both entirely miserable): Mark, the husband, a slave groveling before anyone who might be of use to him in advancing his professional academic career, and Jane, the wife, pinched, testy, and miserable, from having been stereotyped as a woman when what she wanted was to be an intellectual. Both of them are in pell-mell flight from the starkly obvious—from the plain meat-and-potatoes business of being husband and wife to each other as that has been understood and enacted by good and free men and women since the beginning of time.

But that is the trouble. That plain and ancient road is too *bourgeois*. They find their way, or rather their way is found for them, through opposite roads—Mark through Belbury, which is a community in which we may see brought to diabolical fruition all the canons of secular millenarianism; and Jane through St. Anne's, a community where we see dumpy, ordinary people living in purity and harmony and joy because they have learned their lessons well.

The images which Lewis brings to his task in this story are powerful indeed. I have mentioned how Mark and Jane were fending off the ordinary, ancient business of marriage. This is central to Lewis' whole vision. Ordinariness. What we mortals need, he would argue (along with T. S. Eliot), is not the blazing of new trails but rather the grace to walk well the old, plainly marked trails. Sophisticates, who pride themselves in having tried everything (and in being thereby unshockable), are, precisely, *sophisticated*, and to sophisticate something is (OED) "to mix with some foreign or inferior substance; to render impure; to adulterate". It is ironically fitting that we now use the term affirmatively.

In any case, Mark and Jane are sophisticates. The way of salvation for them lies, alas, in walking down, down, down the hill of humility, right down into the valley of ordinariness, where men and women love each other and trust each other and acknowledge their protohistoric need of each other. Mark's salvation from the toils of Belbury lies in his remembering Jane as a woman and as his wife, with her woman's body. He is jolted and rescued by the vision of plain, healthy, stark, external reality when he is about to be traduced utterly by the finely tuned sophistications of Belbury. And we find Jane, again and again, plucked from the toils of her unhappy and sophisticated imagination by the sight of ducks and farmyards and meadows with sunlight on them.

In the moral mythology of C. S. Lewis, the way of health lies along the well-trodden path, not in newly blazed trails. I suppose that if Lewis had lived long enough to see the phenomenon of "happenings" he would have started in horror (he was shockable) at these quite vividly dramatized imaginations of hell. For hell, in Lewis' vision, is the ultimately unstructured place, the place of final fragmentation and randomness and inanity, and this is what was celebrated in the happenings of the 1960s.

The City of God on the other hand (thought Lewis, and Saint Augustine, and Saint John the Divine, and others) is a city four-square, with adamantine foundations and high walls, whose denizens have learned to experience as bliss the steps of the Dance. They are called saints, and their joyful vision of things is wholly remote from what we find extolled in the imagery of contemporaneity. Lewis' works of imagination adumbrate their vision, for if there is one word that rings like the peal of a thousand bells from Lewis' country, it is the word Joy.

CHAPTER TWO

Narnia:
The Forgotten Country

We may call Narnia the forgotten country because far from being a wholly new region, like Magellan's Pacific, or Marco Polo's Cathay, or even the astronauts' moon, it is the very homeland which lies at the back of every man's imagination, which we all yearn for (even if we are wholly unaware of such a yearning), and which has long since disappeared from view in the wake of the vessel we call history. Indeed it is doubly forgotten in that not only have most of us lost any sight or memory of the landscape, but most really modern men, if they came upon a map, or a picture book, or a travelogue describing the land, would put the item aside with a yawn.

The yawn would be a way of saying that the whole topic (that is, the country and its features) was a bore. If some Narnian emissary tried to find out *why* our modern man found the topic boring, he would discover that the features that showed up in the map and the pictures had struck the man as being inconsequential. Trivial even. Childish. The whole panorama held no more interest for him than the panorama of a playroom in a nursery school with its bright blocks, plasticene, and tambourines: nice enough stuff for children, but why are you hailing *me* with this?

To call the land forgotten is to open up a problem of definition, for to say that something is forgotten is to maintain that it was there, once upon a time. If you have forgotten somebody's name, it does not mean that they have no name: rather, there is something faulty about your own powers of holding on to things like names. If you see an old snapshot of yourself at the age of four and exclaim, "My word! I had forgotten those awful shoes they made me clump about in!" the point is not that the shoes never existed but that they did and that your mind, being overburdened with some decades' worth of shoes and other responsibilities, had let the early clodhoppers slip from memory.

But what of Narnia? All these places—Ettinsmoor and Cair Paravel and Lantern Waste and the Lone Islands— surely neither they nor any of these unicorns or centaurs or Marshwiggles, much less these heroic talking mice and sovereign lions, have ever existed in any world that we know anything about!

To say that it was all there, somehow, in the past would seem to be an unlikely view on any accounting. Who will agree with you? Christians and Jews and Muslims will tell you that *that* wasn't the way the holy books describe the beginnings. And scientific materialists and rationalists will tell you that you would be closer to the truth of the matter if you drew some pictures of galactic explosions and lava overflowing and protohistoric mists hovering over fetid bogs. And Jungians, who might allow that a Narnian landscape helps to vivify for us all some very large factors that do seem to lie at the bottom of some sort of universal pool of human consciousness—even they would pause quite under-standably if you became too fervid in urging upon them the notion that Narnia really is a forgotten country.

Perhaps the only people you will convince are children and madmen. With them you might organize a search for the ruins of Cair Paravel somewhere. The rest of us will demur.

How then may we call Narnia a forgotten country? What do we mean when we say that it is there, and that we are exiles who have long since forgotten it? Surely (someone will object) that is to get too solemn. It is to opt out of mature, responsible, contemporary life, and to join the cult of the fantastic along with the organizers of Hobbit Sodalities and Buck Rogers Clubs and Walpurgis Nights. It becomes clear that, if there is any justification for saying that Narnia is a forgotten country, that justification will lie in the region of the imagination.

Ah. The imagination. Of course. Well, that opens the floodgates. Here comes the whole rout of fairies, elves, sprites, gods, goddesses, wights, Peter Pans, Peter Rabbits, March Hares, and so forth. Fun, but nothing much to do with real, serious, authentic modern human existence.

The point here would be, however, that what we encounter in the landscape of Narnia is *true*—not in the sense that we will come upon the ruins of Cair Paravel somewhere (there are none), but rather in the sense that Cair Paravel is a castle, and the man from whose imagination castles have disappeared is disastrously deprived, as is the man who has lost the capacity to appreciate how it can be that for a free man to bow in the presence of a great king, far from being demeaning, is ennobling. This is nonsense, says such a man. But *securus judicat*: the whole world—every tribe and civi-lization for ten thousand years—passes its calm judgment that that is a true thing, and that if under a new and pragmatic mythology that tells us that the way toward our real freedom lies in stirring us all into one grey and undifferentiated pudding where no obedience or veneration is ever due anyone—if under that latter-day outlook there exists an unhappy man who supposes that such a state of affairs is desirable—then (so says the ancient testimony of all human imagination) that man has been deracinated. Uprooted. Exiled. He is living, at best, in a cloud-cuckooland of egalitarian fantasy, and at worst in the grim prison of egalitarian doctrine. For he really does believe that to be free means to be independent and equal with all other creatures, and to have no obligation to do homage to anyone or render obedience to any fixed law, or to take off his shoes in the presence of any sublime imponderables. His world is reasonable, logical, calculated, legal, plausible, political, sifted, and flat. Any pagan, and any Jew or Christian or Hindu or Muslim or animist, would seize his arm and say, "Look: there *are* places where you had best take your shoes off. There *are* taboos. You had better bring sacrifice when you come. You had better pay attention to the bright fixities that preside over your existence."

If, indeed, the real truth about our human life is something like what all religions and mythologies and tribes and civilizations until about two hundred years ago have suspected, then the stories that tell us about life in those terms would seem to be not misleading but true. Or, to put it more cautiously, they are at least as true, for all of their unicorns and trumpets and spells, as the stories (e.g., post-seventeenth-century European and American fiction) that speak of human experience as though no news had come in from the outside, and as though no one has ever found himself hailed with mystery and glory and dread that loom upon him and that defy his attempts to find manageable explanations for them.

The tales of Narnia open up to us a certain kind of world. It is a world which has been made—made by Someone, beautifully made. Its fabric is shot through with glory. There is no peak, no valley, no sea or forest, but bears the weight of this glory; no law of the land that does not mirror the exact pattern of this glory; no spell or incantation or taboo that does not reach through the veil that protects the mundane and the obvious from the great glories and mysteries that press upon them; no creature—no faun, dryad, star, or winged horse—that does not bear about and exhibit in its own form some bit of the shape of that glory. And, alas, there is no evil that does not turn out to be fraud, parody, or counterfeit of that glory. In every case, the appeal of evil in Narnia springs from illusion and leads eventually to sterility, destruction, and anger.

Now, if that is the sort of world which the "fairy" chronicles of Narnia open up to us, it turns out to be a world identical in every significant point with the world that all myths and religions have told us we live in. Taken item for item, at least up to this point, Narnia turns out to be indistinguishable from the world that the sages and seers and saints and druids and prophets have thought they saw. Indeed we could with no difficulty translate these items into the language of Jewish and Christian sacred texts. "It is a world which has been made—made by Someone" becomes Genesis 1. "No peak, no valley ... but bears the weight of this glory" becomes Psalm 19. "No law of the land that does not mirror the exact pattern of this glory" becomes Psalm 119. The story of evil as fraud and illusion is told in Genesis. And so forth.

The point of all this is that if we find the chronicles of Narnia to be inconsequential in their subject matter, then the world pictured by all myths and religions is inconsequential.

But two cautions arise here. First, the fact that these chronicles speak of that sort of world does not thereby make them good books. You can have terrible books about sublime things. One of the questions at work in the present book is whether or not we may call these *books* good. This question is distinct from the question as to whether we happen to like or believe in the sort of *world* evoked in Lewis' works.

And second, if we were to claim that there is a significant correspondence between Narnia and the real world, then we have opened up the troublesome topic of allegory, and everyone is off chasing parallels. Aslan equals Christ; the White Witch equals Lilith; Peter equals Saint Peter, and so forth.

Lewis himself dispelled this line of thought. He did not set out to write something like *The Pilgrim's Progress*, in which we may discover one-for-one correspondences between the characters and images in the story and people or conditions in our own world, so that Christian *equals* you and me on pilgrimage to heaven, and the Giant Despair equals despair, and so forth. That is allegory, but the connection between what we find in Narnia and anything in our own story is closer to analogy, where we say, not "Aslan equals Christ", but rather, "As Christ is to this story, so, in a measure, is Aslan to that one." It is at least partly the difference between *symbols* and *cases in point*, which we run into every day. You may see a boy offer to carry a grocery bag for a woman. He is not a symbol of Christ (carrying someone else's burden): rather, he appears in this little act as a case in point of the same thing which was also at work in Christ's act, namely Charity, which always "substitutes" itself for the good of someone else. That is, both the boy with the groceries, and Calvary, are cases in point of this Charity. The boy is not a symbol: he really is enacting and exhibiting Charity, the supreme case in point of which is Calvary. (We need not here settle the question as to the exact relation between his act and Christ's except to say that somehow, in the Christian view, acts like this boy's may be "taken into", or "made part of", Christ's One Offering. The boy *adds* nothing to that Offering; but on the other hand his act is indeed "added to" that Offering in the mystery whereby God takes our human flesh into his purposes [cf. such mysteries as the body of Mary becoming the vehicle for the Incarnation, or the Church as Christ's Body being privileged to participate in his priesthood].)

Thus we make a mistake if we try to chase symbols up and down the landscape of Narnia, or if we try to pin down allegories. It is much better to read these tales for what they are, namely fairy tales. We blunder sadly if we try to read them as anything else—as cryptograms or anagrams or acrostics for Christian theology and morals.

Of course no one, least of all Lewis himself, can fend off the inevitable: we are going, willy-nilly, to see creatures and situations in Narnia that remind us of our own story. But this happens in all kinds of stories: Achilles, for example, sulks and becomes jealous and furious and grieved, and we recognize these states of mind all too well; and as we find them at work in a godlike and heroic figure like Achilles, somehow the whole enterprise of being human, and of being prey to tumultuous emotions, takes on much greater weight and clarity for us than it might have had if we were left to muddle along with our own private and rather murky feelings. We are the sort of creature (as opposed, say, to dogs or angels) who need not only to *go through* experiences but to go through them once more, or a thousand times more, by telling them back to ourselves and thus getting some distance and leverage on them. As long as I can only howl about my grief, or writhe over my jealousy, or fume out my wrath, I am *under* the experience and not master of it. As soon as I can step back a bit and get hold of it, either by articulating it myself, or by someone else's doing this for me (say, a poet), then I begin to be freed from its tyranny. I am helped to be what a mortal man is supposed to be, namely a creature who rules his passions and who makes choices in the light of more than these mere passions.

But if we come at Homer's epic about Achilles with our analytic loins all girded up, ready with pencil and clipboard to sketch out all sorts of complicated parallels between Achilles and ourselves, or to list like groceries Homer's "insights" into "the human condition", then we are like a man drinking a glass of wine who talks only of alcohol count in the bloodstream or how you go about bottling this elixir: the rest of us want to shout at him to desist and drink up. What about the *taste*? What about the *pleasure*? You can get alcohol into your blood in all sorts of ways; and you can put any liquid into a bottle. But how do you like the taste of *this*? By the same token, we read Homer's epic not primarily to discover insights but to have the experience of *reading an epic*. And if we want to do this, we must understand that it is an epic we have embarked upon and not a novel, much less a text in psychology or morals. This makes a great deal of difference, for if we confuse it with a novel, for example, then we will quarrel with Homer for not having written long paragraphs on the subtle interplay of Achilles' various feelings. The trouble here is that long paragraphs about the subtle interplay of feelings belong only in one kind of narrative, namely the modern psychological novel. We don't want them in either the tale of Achilles or of Peter Rabbit, since neither of these tales draws primarily upon psychological analysis for its substance (there may be more insights in those tales than one will find in most textbooks, but neither Homer nor Beatrix Potter had that sort of thing in mind when they put their tales together). To ask for this sort of thing in an epic or a fairy tale is like asking why someone doesn't fill in all the wasted space in a cathedral by putting in ten stories: think how many secretaries could be accommodated. The suggestion makes enormous good sense from the standpoint of heating costs and conviviality and efficient use of space, but it does not make sense *here*. If a cathedral is anything at all, it is lofty. Let us either have lofty cathedrals or none. But let us not talk of filling them in. There is the Empire State Building for that sort of thing.

So, when we are reading a fairy tale (which is what the Narnian chronicles are) we must accept the special terms of the fairy tale, as we do those of a cathedral.

But this picture of the cathedral raises a certain question about fairy tales. We are not sure that anyone nowadays ought to be building cathedrals, at least immense ones—there is no harm in having the bishop's chair in a church. These noble edifices were exactly appropriate to a certain vision of things at work for some hundreds of years of history in Europe. The vision (of glory, of mystery, of sanctity) that begot the cathedrals is no longer abroad in the land, so if we find someone proposing to raise money for a new one, we say, "No: put the money into urban planning or hunger relief." The idea in our objection is that such a building is a grotesque anachronism in the world as we know it now.

Some such notion would also be at work in the suspicion with which "official" criticism might tend to look at Lewis' fairy tales. They are anachronisms, especially *these* fairy tales, full as they are of otiose ideas like majesty and fixed morality and so forth.

This is a question that applies to almost any form of art. Can we write epics now? Or romances? Should we even try? Is it possible today to compose opera—real opera—or was that an eighteenth- and nineteenth-century phenomenon, like baroque or Georgian architecture? What about sonnets? What about portraits and still lifes? Are they still valid? Or what about the big topics the painters used to treat—the Annunciation, say?

In all of these questions we find ourselves on the tricky frontier between life and art. One of the difficulties on that frontier is to decide whether art—the poetry and the plays and the paintings—is supposed merely to reflect truthfully what our experience *is*, or whether it must also keep hailing us with things we may have forgotten. Does a poet, for example, shape into words the experiences of his generation, using the imagery that is very close at hand; or does he also, at some point, have the task of flagging down his generation and saying, "Ahoy! Over this way! You're headed the wrong direction. Here's a whole world you have forgotten."

The poetry of T. S. Eliot in the twentieth century is a good case in point of this. In his "Prufrock" he caught exactly the boredom and impotence of the century, and he put it all in terms that were frighteningly familiar: drains, ether, shirtsleeves, cigarette butts, and so forth. No silver trumpets or heroes there. But later in his life he undertook the daunting task of trying to speak to this same century about topics that it not only was wholly ignorant of, but that it had lost the capacity even to imagine, namely sanctity, felicity, and the Eternal Word made flesh in time. He spoke of these things in his *Four Quartets*, not because he thought his audience would snap up the poetry eagerly, but because he saw his poet's task as being something like the prophet's, namely, to speak of what is *true*, whether there are any ears about to hear it or not.

It was an ordeal for him, both in his later poetry and in his drama. In the *Four Quartets* he even speaks of the struggle itself in such lines as "That was a way of putting it—not very satisfactory.... Leaving one still with the intolerable wrestle / With words and meanings. The poetry does not matter." [1]

What was this struggle? Surely it was at least partly the struggle which is almost unique to artists in our own century, the struggle to speak about what poets and artists have always extolled—beauty, perfection, felicity—to a generation whose eyes and ears are so diseased that not only have they heard no news at all from a far country, but their eyes and ears are now incapable of receiving such news. How do you talk of light to a bat? How do you speak of the sea to a scorpion in the Sahara? How do you tell a tapeworm about eagles' flight? In each case you would have the awful job of beginning with something that the creature knew, and of nudging him along toward something he had never in his wildest imaginings conceived of.

In his *Four Quartets*, Eliot begins with pictures which he hopes we may recognize—a door into a rose garden, children playing, a dried-up pool; but before long, he is pushing us away from these familiar things, and he finds that he must show us mediaeval tapestries, and try to suggest something that we may not have thought of: namely that there just might be some connection between our lymph systems and the movement of the stars. A pattern, in other words. A cosmic design or tapestry, say, or even a dance, in which

[1] T. S. Eliot, *Four Quartets*, "East Coker" (New York: Harcourt Brace Jovanovich, 1943, 1971), pp. 25, 26.

everything steps in time with everything else, and moves
out into one harmonious pattern of adoration.

But by this time we have been dragged right away from
the dried-up pools and other workaday plausibilities and
are being hailed with the sort of thing an Isaiah or a Saint
Augustine or a Dante might have hailed us with. The absurdity here is that Eliot is a *twentieth-century* poet, and it looks
suspiciously like an attempt on his part to dodge the tough
realities of modern life and to hide amongst Old Testament
or mediaeval bric-a-brac. Actually, modern criticism has had
to take up one of three attitudes toward Eliot: 1) embarrassed: "Why do you suppose Eliot is so galvanized by all
that?"; 2) avuncular: "Oh well, poor Tom Eliot's gone right
off into religious masochism"; or 3) urbane: "Of course what
Eliot is actually speaking of under his peculiar mystic imagery is what we all agree on anyway, namely the ambiguity
of living in time." In each case Eliot's assault on us is blunted.
Very few critics have been known to drop his book, leap
from their chairs in terror, and fly to the confessional to be
shriven.

I have spoken at length of Eliot's work here, not to advance
the idea that Lewis' achievement in his fairy tales was like,
or equal to, Eliot's achievement in his poetry, but rather
because in both cases we find twentieth-century writers trying to speak of things that no one has heard of, or that
everyone has forgotten, or that no one takes seriously any
longer. Eliot attempts it by pushing us and pushing us, insisting that we ourselves press through to what is hinted at and
glimpsed fleetingly in every experience that lies around us
(he even speaks of these "hints and guesses"), his idea, finally,
being of course that what is hinted at is nothing other than
Glory. But by the time he gets us there he has long since
been obliged to introduce us to Dante and the Lady Julian

and Saint John of the Cross, because our modern vocabulary bears no witness at all to the fixities they bore witness
to, namely sanctity, felicity, and the Incarnation. Lewis makes
a different sort of attempt, which we have already described
in terms of an invitation to a shuttered window in the dark
and stuffy room in which we are trapped, where he bursts
the shutters open and shouts, "Look! Look out there!" And
what he shows us out there is a landscape—a landscape in
which we may see all sorts of terrors and glories that we
had never dreamed of, trapped in the dark of our prison.

For Eliot (or Lewis) to do this sort of thing is as odd as
for a major twentieth-century painter to take up such subjects as the Annunciation. It is all very well for pious enter-
prises sponsored by convents or religious publishing houses
who want illustrations for Sunday school materials. But we
do not expect to find this sort of thing coming from our
serious painters. If a Picasso, or even an Andrew Wyeth,
did so, we would all be murmuring, "Why do you suppose
he's gone back to that?"

But if we asked ourselves why we were made suspicious
here, we would have to answer that the Annunciation is
not considered to be a serious or "viable" bit of subject
matter in our century, and that therefore a recognized artist
who took it up must be taunting us, or fiddling, or else
toying with his own technique. One could hardly conceive
that he was actually serious about the Annunciation or
thought this subject as important as any clown or any field
in Chadds Ford that he might paint.

And if an Eliot or a Dante or a Saint Augustine pressed
the question on us, insisting that we tell him why the Annunciation seems so inconsequential to us, we would have to
cast about and mumble something about the world having
got beyond all that, and about technology and war and the

scientific outlook and realism and one thing and another, not one syllable of which would make the slightest sense to either Dante or Saint Augustine (Eliot would at least understand, even though he would disagree with us).

"You mean you don't think your world has been visited?"

"Visited?"

"Your existence has not been hailed with glory?"

"Hailed with what?"

"Glory."

"There is no such thing."

"You think the poets and sages and prophets and saints were whistling in the dark then?"

"Oh well, now, you must understand ..."

"They were wrong then. The god has never come. Is that it?"

"Well, we look at things scientifically. Those are great poetical constructs ..."

"You have heard no news from outside, then?"

"Well, we have very sophisticated satellites and antennae ..."

"No news, though. Is that it?"

Our original question about the painter betrays everything: "Why do you suppose he's gone *back* to that?" Back. There is the great problem in one syllable: have we gone forward, meaning *toward* a view of life that is more accurate than the view that filled paintings and poetry with gods and heroes and angels, or have we not? On one side of the question stands the modern world. On the other stands the witness of millennia of poetry, prophecy, and sanctity. But that problem is not our primary concern here. Ours is the poet's problem: how does a poet or a painter or storyteller who finds himself living and working in this century—how does he propose to speak of such topics as sanctity or felicity without going *back*? That is, what materials can he work up from the familiar world of contemporary experience to show us what he wants to show us? We have drains and cigarette butts, and these have been put to good use in the iconography of the last eighty years. And we have tramps who wait for Godot, and streetcars, and glass menageries and bald sopranos and hairy apes. But if you want to speak of something *else* what do you do?

The trouble here of course is over this "something else" that an Eliot (or a Mauriac or a Flannery O'Connor or an Auden or a Rouault) wants to speak of. It would be all very well if this "else"—this other vision that seems so alien and unyielding—were something that you could take or leave, like a fascination for cuneiform or herb gardens or flying saucers. But what if you (the poet) think it is crucial? What if you think it is not just crucial but *Everything*? And more than that: what if your view is not just a private conviction of your own, but is shared by Judaism and Greek antiquity and Christianity and Islam and every animistic tribe to boot? What if you find that no one had any other root idea until very, very recently? And what if you (and all the sages and poets that you can rake up) think that this recent shift was a disaster? Then what do you do? What language will you choose in which to lift up your voice in the streets? What pictures will you display by way of show-and-tell? What bright banners will you unfurl? What heraldry will you blazon?

Heraldry. There's the rub. Sooner or later you are going to have to resort to pictures that look strange to these shopkeepers and shoppers in *Vanity Fair*. They know all about merchandise and prices and distribution and one thing and another. But they do not know about lions rampant. They have not heard about unicorns. But you want to tell them about these lions and unicorns not to divert or trick them but to wake them up to the awful fact that there is a lion ramping upon them, and to the blissful fact that there is ineffably sweet and noble purity galloping over the downs somewhere. You have, in other words, to reach *back* for your pictures, since nothing seems to be lying about that suggests quite what you want to suggest.

The poets come at this problem in different ways, of course. Eliot reached for Dante and the Celestial Rose—hardly your average modern image. Flannery O'Connor came at it by artistic default, so to speak: she drew grotesqueries in her fiction, but to everyone's discomfiture her most grotesque characters turn out to be the ones who have some hint in their fevered brains about sanctity and glory. The normal, modern, civilized ones are the brutes. We may call this technique "default" because she tried to remind us of sanctity not by pointing directly to it but to what you get without it. And it is worth noting in her case that when she does want to speak explicitly of sanctity or grace or glory (all items that her readers would be wholly unfamiliar with), she must introduce an old Irish priest who unapologetically and eccentrically burrs away about the Second Coming or the Eucharist—ancient Catholic orthodoxy, in other words. She had to reach back.

Another writer in our time who has made the odd attempt to reach away from the drains and cigarette butts is Lewis' friend Tolkien. His ploy was to step across the border into a land which we cannot locate either in our history or our geography. And yet paradoxically there does seem to be some remote connection with our history at least. Tolkien makes his great tale occur in the "Third Age of Middle Earth", drawing on the picture from Northern mythology, in which our earth is known as "Midgard"—middle earth. To that extent he has planted his tale deep in the soil of Western imagination. But he has created his own set of situations and creatures, especially hobbits. When we read this saga, we find ourselves regaled with visions of fear and bliss that tower far above most of what we encounter in "realistic" fiction. We find at work in that world such notions as majesty and mystery and purity and nobility and taboo and heroism and so forth—all of which we tend to attach to "antiquity", and none of which we run across in modern fiction for the obvious reason that the modern novel concerns itself with the modern world and the modern world has great difficulty taking those old notions seriously. If these notions crop up anywhere in the modern world, they find themselves hurried into the category "religion" or "the occult" or some other category safely sealed away from the real stream of modern life.

Once more, the obvious irony is that these notions that are so much at work in Tolkien's Middle Earth, far from being private fantasies of his, are the very notions that all myths and all religions have supposed formed the real fabric of our real existence. In other words, from that point of view it would be impossible to tell any true stories about human existence without taking these notions into account. Not that Dickens ought to have had angels flitting through his London alleyways or that Tolstoy should have had Dmitri Karamazov run into a troll somewhere. Rather, the question might be put this way, as though it were being asked of the modern world by the whole long lineage of poets and tellers of tales: "If you (the people who live in the West after the eighteenth century) are going to confine your narratives to what you call 'realism', and not even allow the sort of narrative that the human race told itself for thousands of years, how complete and clear a picture of human experience will you be able to get?"

Our answer of course will be to trot out the major story-tellers of our era: Jane Austen, George Eliot, Dickens, Tolstoy, Flaubert, Henry James, D. H. Lawrence, and the rest, and to say, "Well, there is the record. Doesn't that speak for itself?"

And our senate of poets and prophets would scrutinize it all and they would have to nod in awe at the beauty and magnitude of this achievement. But then we would see them put their heads together, with a great deal of mumbling and scratching and wagging of heads, and a spokesman would stand up and ask, "But is this *all* you wish to speak of in your tales? Do you think these stories quite catch all that is at work in your experience? We are puzzled. No character in any one of these tales ever seems to blunder into any sacred grove. None of them is cut down by the gods. No one ever comes upon holiness, or wrestles with sin. No one receives grace. How can you tell really true stories if you leave all that out?"

And some able critic from among us would have to rise and point out to the venerable gentlemen that the real truth of our experience in the modern world is that life does, in fact, proceed with no reference to such things as holiness and sin and grace. Or, if he is very urbane, he will point out that what the old tellers of tales *meant* when they dotted their landscapes with grottoes and sacred groves, and when they peopled their tales with gods and fauns, is the very thing *we* mean when we have our characters struggle with certain psychological conundrums. We think it is closer to the truth of the matter if we speak of a character reaching maturity, or coming to grips with his problems, than if we have him being turned into a stag by the gods or reaching home after a long odyssey. But (we would urge) the picture of Ulysses' long voyage and that of Isabel Archer's progress toward maturity both furnish us with accurate accounts of exactly the same thing. It is just that we would not be faithful to modern experience if we showed our characters wrestling with the gods, since the gods have turned out to be nothing more than worthy and useful fictions—projections of currents and forces that seem to lie inside of us, not outside.

Inside and outside. Here is a crux like the crux we came upon with heraldry. Where is the real landscape? Shall we assign everything to the interior? Is our mental and emotional landscape the only one there is? Are the gods and the titans fighting only in our brains and lymph systems? Is the scene of conflict really the parlor after all, and not the walls of Troy? Is the pit only my despondence and not really Acheron?

We cannot think about these things for very long without reaching one of two points of view: either the landscape and hence the struggle is all inside, or *it is both inside and outside.* (No one, presumably, could possibly take up the third view, namely, that the conflict occurs *only* outside of us: you cannot be alive and be unaware that wherever else the struggle may be going on, it is certainly going on inside of you.) The big watershed in human imagination must have appeared only very lately in history when the West decided that if anything were outside (which is unverifiable) it is in any event unknowable and that therefore we will ignore it. Philosophers and historians can track this watershed to the Enlightenment, or to the Renaissance, or even its lower slopes to the latter Middle Ages. They can assign the credit (or blame) for its discovery to David Hume or Immanuel Kant, or, pushing things back further, to Peter Ramus or even Aristotle. However we wish to describe it and wherever we wish to locate it finally, its effect on imagination is stark: either we live inside a bag that is hermetically sealed from whatever is (or more probably isn't) outside of it; or we really do live "outside", in the world that the poets and prophets supposed they saw. We (moderns) suppose of course that they *didn't* see what they thought they saw, that it was all mirage, and that we have reduced everything to amino acids and DNA. We may still read what they wrote, but we will not suppose that they wrote about what they thought they were writing about. *We* know what they were writing about (emotional conflicts, not gods and titans), but they didn't.

Now at this point someone who knows a thing or two about the history of human imagination is going to point out, quite correctly, that far from really believing in all those gods that they wrote about, even the ancient poets (Homer and Ovid and Virgil for example) were probably only "telling tales". And, *a fortiori*, certainly Eliot does not suppose Ultimate Reality looks like a rose, nor does Tolkien expect to find hobbits in Oxfordshire, nor Lewis unicorns in Cambridgeshire. Aren't you introducing a false or at least a factitious dichotomy into things here? Isn't it all a question of mere imagery?

Not quite. On one level of course, it is. A man who really does think that we live in this sealed bag may decide that he would like to have some gods in his story, and he may put them to good use. And by the same token a man who really does think that the universe is wide open, and who wonders what celestial and infernal traffic hurries up and down, may decide to restrict his tale to the parlor. On this level we have simply the question of imagery: where shall I locate my tale—Asgard or London?

But if we press the business further we will discover that the question about imagery leads us back to the prior one about the sort of world we live in. *Is* there anything outside? If so, can we know anything about it? And will we discover it by séances and black masses, or by sending satellites out toward Uranus? If there is nothing, or if contact is impossible, may we nonetheless pretend that there is by populating our stories with gods and fauns? Or better yet, may we talk of our interior experience by means of these gods and fauns, never for a moment fooling ourselves that this machinery is anything other than a fanciful but useful device to help us vivify our own experience?

One way of getting a clear picture of this watershed is to ask two authors which sort of story seems to come closest to catching the truth about our mortal existence, since that is what all stories are ultimately about. One may say, "Well, I think our existence is more like what you find in the modern novel", and the other, "I suppose our existence is more like what you find in fairy tales." More like. What is our story *like*?

This may bring us back to Tolkien, and thence to Lewis. Tolkien, like most poets and tellers of tales for some thousands of years, really did suppose that our story is very like a fairy tale, not because he was a sentimentalist (he was very crusty) but because he believed that this world is like that. However, that is not why he wrote the stories he wrote. He wrote them because he happened to like that kind of story, not because he wanted to smuggle out a tract that would reintroduce the religious view into everyone's imagination. He fought off quite fiercely any suggestion that his saga had any ulterior purpose. He was a storyteller in the old tradition of the bards who sang to us because this is a worthy and beautiful thing to do. If you want propaganda, even propaganda for the gods, then by all means have it; but do not ask me to write your propaganda, Tolkien seems to say.

On the other hand Tolkien not only thought that the real, sober truth about our mortal existence is like a fairy tale: he also argued the point in his long essay "On Fairy Stories". Being a Catholic, he thought that the cold truth of the matter was that these haunting mysteries and odd taboos that beleaguer our life and bedevil our imaginations have their origin not in our guts but in the empyrean. It is deity who says, "Thus far and no farther", not merely society. It is against principalities and powers that we fight, not against mere social injustice.

On this accounting then we may not quite conclude that Sauron is a successful and terrifying projection of forces that we mortals all know within ourselves. That may be so: but if Sauron is *like* anything, he is like something that was outside of us before it came inside. It was not spawned in our entrails. Or again, Gandalf and Aragorn are noble images of power and goodness that anyone may recognize, but if we want to track down why images like this ring all sorts of bells in our imaginations we shall have to look further than inside those imaginations: we shall have to look out, to the sort of world our story occurs in. There is Saint Michael the Archangel (Tolkien might say) before there is my wish for a glorious warrior. There is the hidden king and heir before there is my longing that he come into his inheritance.

But Tolkien boils into the breach here shouting, "No allegories! No allegories!" And he is right. Gandalf is not the archangel and Aragorn is not the Messiah. But on the other hand, there is a Story which has archangels and a "sent one"—and real titanic conflict into which great and small alike are swept—and all true stories will somehow resonate with the echoes from that Story, since in Tolkien's view that is the only story there is, finally. How do you make your story true? Or put it another way: what sort of story is a true story? What are you likely to encounter in a true story?

We may come at an answer to some of these questions by remarking on the sort of thing we encounter in the landscape of Narnia and the action that we find occurring there. Since the nature of fairy tales is to proceed simply and without apology from one event to the next, it may be that the most useful method of observing what Lewis is up to in these narratives, and the method most faithful to the special technique (if we may give it as cold a name as technique) of fairy tale, is simply to move along the path of the narrative noting what we see and subordinating the "criticism" of fairy tales to the apparently simple pattern of that kind of narrative, rather than to try to force them into the Procrustean bed of, say, the modern novel with the highly structural analysis that is appropriate to that kind of narrative.

There are literally thousands of observations that may be made as one moves along through the landscape of faerie. The following would seem to be at least some of the features worth noting in the land called Narnia, since they not only suggest to us the sort of world in which we find ourselves in these narratives, but also seem to set up resonances with the story, giving us our most important clue as to the nature of Lewis' achievement in these tales.

For one thing, we do not get very far before we discover that it is Lucy who ordinarily seems to see things first. Again and again, whether it is the very first discovery of Narnia beyond the wardrobe, or the first glimpse of Aslan, she has the gift of recognition. If we read far enough in Lewis we will find a theme, hinted at in this small beginning in Narnia, of womanhood as being especially receptive to the approaches of mystery or glory, or the divine, say. We see this in Mrs. Beaver's instant response to the appearance of the four children. " 'So you've come at last!' she said, holding out both her wrinkled old paws. 'At last! To think that ever I should live to see this day!' " (Who can avoid hearing old Anna waiting in the temple with Simeon?) Tinidril, Jane Studdock, Psyche, and Orual herself: they all *see* things.

Then, the image of the "feminine" *eldil* Perelandra, and indeed the very texture of the landscape in the planet Perelandra, warm and fluid, suggest fecundity and nourishment— those qualities brought into play in response to the planting of some seed. Lewis, of course, knew and believed the story in which the figure called upon to respond to the approach of the god was a woman. Her flesh and indeed her very womanhood seemed to be the type and image of all human life as that life stands over against the divine life. What, in that story, is the proper response of that flesh to the approach of the divine? "Be it unto me according to thy word." Either this, or bitterness and desolation.

Again we may note that the narrative returns with more than random recurrence to scenes where we find cups of tea or tankards of beer, and cakes and sandwiches, or a fireside and pipes and hot baths and so forth. Frequently we find this sort of interlude either en route to some great crux in the action or just after some great peril or victory. It is always very commonplace stuff, and that is the whole point. It is a theme right at the center of all of Lewis' vision: simplicity, good fellowship, the goodness of creation, the sheer pleasure of good tastes and smells and textures—fresh bread, raspberries, nuts—even the lowly bean which Lewis lauds in one poem. What are all wars and all economics and all politics about? Do they not all come down in the end to the business of allowing people to return to their hearthsides and to family and friends and good fellowship? What would all exiles and all prisoners and all dying people sell their souls to regain if not these highest pleasures— pleasures mediated to us under the lowly species of tea and cakes and laughter and fondling? In the fairy tale landscape of Narnia we see this recurrently.

And in this connection we may note the place of sheer festivity and merrymaking in Narnia. Here we come upon dancing and drinking and the congregating of many different *sorts* of creatures: dwarfs, fauns, dryads, rabbits, foxes, badgers, centaurs, giants, dogs, and humans. It is clear that the very pattern in the fabric of this world depends on threads of many different colors and materials—very like the pattern in the fabric of the world that stood as the backdrop to Lewis' whole imagination, namely the world in which all things in their varied shapes and colors—*omnia opera Domini*—dance and sing: from warriors and seraphim to rabbits and foxes and badgers, with heroes and charwomen and cabbies and all.

With respect to these rabbits and other amiable and harmless-looking small creatures in Narnia, we may observe in Lewis' narrative art what he called "good unoriginality". That is, it seems to be fixed in our imaginations that rabbits and bluebirds and deer are not only harmless but good, so that for a storyteller (Lewis commends Disney for this) to assume all these well-worn suppositions on our part is much better than for him to wrench things about and catch us off guard with villainous tomtits or blackguardly lambs. They *look* harmless and trustworthy, so at least for our story let us assume that our imaginations are leading us in the right direction. In Narnia, for example, when the four children find themselves being led along by a robin, Edmund, who it may be recalled is out of sympathy with everything, complains that they have no way of knowing whose side this bird is on. Whereupon Peter, always to be trusted for the right point of view, comments crisply that every robin in any story *he* knows anything about is good.

The point is that these images are some sort of trustworthy index of something that is real. When Edmund and the Witch see a squirrel with his wife and family, with two satyrs, a dwarf, and a fox, sitting on stools at a table eating a plum pudding that has been decorated with holly, it is quite clear to them and to us that something good is afoot, which of course infuriates the Witch. You don't find things like *that* about without suspecting something good. And when the children hear the jingling bells and see the sledge of Father Christmas, it is abundantly clear that good *is* abroad, since sledges and jingling bells spell joy. (The Witch also had a sledge with bells—but that is the very point: hers was a counterfeit, exactly like the real thing but a cheat. Evil can only parody goodness; it cannot invent new forms of real beauty and joy. That is why in fairy tales you have to beware of attractive disguises—nice old crones selling apples in the forest, say, or angels of light.)

There are variations on the theme of festivity. Sometimes it takes the form of merrymaking and sheer jollity; and at other times it is solemn—equally joyous, but solemn. Festal pomp, with gravity and ceremony presiding over all, seems somehow to be in the cards. When Aslan crowns Peter, or when he sings Narnia into being, or bestows speech on the animals who are to be Talking Beasts, there is a hush in the air, and solemnity, that gives us a glimpse of the other face of joy. The expectant motionlessness on the one hand, and the great clamorous rush of all the creatures up into the final Narnia, are the *largo* and the *vivace* of joy, we might say.

Once or twice we hear passing tidings of a Milk-white Stag that is seen only at immensely infrequent intervals on the marches of Narnia. It seems to have almost nothing to do with the plot, but it sounds a note, like old Triton's horn, or like the casements opening on faerie seas forlorn, that haunt us with fugitive beauty. Apparently Narnia is the sort of place where, whatever beauties you may see, there are still more and others, beyond the borders of your ken. Though yours is a story full of joys and terrors, it is not the only story. There are beauties that would burst your heart if you encountered them now, and terrors that would wither you utterly. You may catch hints of them, but they are not part of your story for the moment. Lewis, of course, thought that something like this was true of all possible stories.

The evil which is abroad in Narnia when we first come into the land takes the form of a White Witch. We learn from Mr. Beaver that she is of the race of Lilith, Adam's first wife, according to an old and persistent legend. Because of dissatisfaction and disobedience on her part, she was driven into exile, and Eve took her place as the mother of mankind. For this reason, Lilith hates fruitfulness and love and the honest intercourse of man with woman. She is the archetype of all wicked fairies who show up at cradles and christenings, and her particular ploy is illusion. If she can lull you and entice you away from light-of-day reality, and lead you into the sterile limbo of illusion where you will dry up and die, then she has done what she wants to do. She is Lamia, and *la belle dame sans merci*, and the Green Witch of *The Silver Chair*, and all others like this. She is always attractive, almost irresistible; to resist her takes every ounce of moral fortitude, every device of memory that you can summon to help you recall what *was* true no matter what deception she now blinds you with. Edmund is siphoned off into Judaslike treachery by the simple offer of Turkish delight; Prince Rilian is held in a deathlike thrall by Lilith and her ilk.

The greatest fear of these witches is that sons of Adam and daughters of Eve will show up. Human flesh is their greatest hate, as it is Satan's (cf. *Paradise Lost*), for human flesh is the jewel in the crown of the Enemy; human flesh is the heir of the land which the Witch holds in her thrall. (We find that Narnia is only truly itself, and its denizens truly free and safe, if humans are on the Four Thrones at Cair Paravel; apparently some sort of sovereignty is to be borne and exercised for the good of all by *human* flesh, not by fauns or lions or dryads elected by majority vote.) Human flesh is the sign of real joy, since it enacts in itself the intelligent Dance of Charity, where self-giving equals ecstasy (sex and the marriage sacrament is the great physical metaphor of this); and human flesh is the agent of the final victory over all falsehood and illusion and fraud. In another Story this all follows the sequence: Annunciation-Nativity-Passion-Resurrection-Ascension-Apocalypse. Flesh is the very sign of the *other*, which Lilith hates, but which is the desire and object of Charity. In the image of the Dance we see the one mode of flesh (woman) answering to the other mode (man). Antiphons of joy. Sheer, blissful Fact. It is Fact that stands over against the blandishments and illusions of hell—or of Lilith.

Over against all this dimness stands the wry and merry wisdom of Professor Kirke which in its rare appearances in the narrative furnishes a sort of standard by which we may test what is going on. It is as though he is *there*, like the duke in *Measure for Measure*, or the prince in *Romeo and Juliet*, not as a major character in the action, but as a reference point, the embodiment of order and goodness. It may not be for nothing that Lewis has named him Kirke: we have seen this motif before in the figure of Mother Kirk

in *The Pilgrim's Regress*. And Lewis' own mentor Mac-
Donald was a Scot, in whose native land they call the Church
the Kirk. Professor Kirke has been to school in Aslan's country (see *The Magician's Nephew*: Kirke is Digory), and has
learned the hard lessons of plain obedience, and of trusting
against all odds that Aslan knows what he is doing, and of
not being too sure what *can't* happen, and of the paradoxes
at work in the country of Charity, where every man feeds
on the fruit plucked by another's labor, and so forth. So
that when the children bring their quarrel about Lucy's absurd
report on the wardrobe to him, his question is, "How do
you know that your sister's story is not true?" And his advice
to all of them, learned no doubt from long lessons, is, "We
might all try minding our own business." In another place,
where everyone asks how on earth these wonders can be,
we hear the Professor muttering to himself, "What do they
teach schoolchildren these days", since "it's all in Plato".

Here we find a note struck that is important to Lewis'
vision, and for which Lewis had venerable precedent in
Spenser and Milton, namely the assumption that pagan wisdom and mythology may furnish us with some very significant clues to things. Spenser, in his Christian epic on Charity,
The Faerie Queene, takes us to such pagan haunts as the Cave
of Morpheus and the Garden of Adonis. Milton calls Christ
Pan in his hymn for the Nativity. In Narnia we find Silenus
and Bacchus themselves, surely the most pagan of all pagan
gods, with their vines and wreaths and capering and tip-
pling. And Plato. All of this in a narrative that takes us into
a country that we are finally obliged to recognize as *like* the
country longed for in the Psalms of the Hebrews and the
vision of Saint John the Divine.

But is not that country the very antithesis of all pagan
countries? No, says Lewis (and Milton, and Spenser, and all

Renaissance Christian humanists). Rather, put it this way: that Country is the country hinted at and guessed at and dreamed of and longed for in *all* tales of joy and merriment and homecoming and reunion and harmony. Arcadia and the Garden of the Hesperides and the land of the Hyperboreans and Narnia and all of the other places are like "good dreams". To be sure, often the shafts of light from the real Country fall on the "jungle of filth and imbecility" that is, alas, our imagination, all ridden as it is with cupidity and concupiscence, so that you get chaos and lechery and perfidy romping through the stories. But back of it all shimmers the dream of primaeval and everlasting bliss, and the aching desire for that bliss.

Early in the narrative we come upon a small exchange that opens onto an enormous watershed. The children find that Mr. Tumnus the faun has been taken prisoner by the Witch's police, and it seems that his crime has been his hospitality to Lucy. Lucy protests that they must do something—after all, mere decency would dictate that. Susan and Peter agree, and Edmund objects. As it happens they decide to see what they can do, and on this decision hangs the entire tale. This sort of unobtrusive, even minuscule, juncture in the action, which later turns out to be not only important but crucial, and even, on hindsight, a matter of obedience or disobedience to the voice of Aslan himself—this occurs again and again in these fairy tales.

But what is at work in Narnia that makes this sort of crux plausible is the same sort of judgment that hangs like a canopy over our own story: great things hanging upon apparently insignificant decisions, and the whole weight of responsibility for the great things attaching to those small choices. Abraham pulling up stakes and leaving Ur—and becoming the father of the faithful thereby. The Good Samaritan turning out of his way just for a minute—and becoming for all of history the paradigm of Charity. And all the alarming language about "inasmuch as ye did it unto one of the least of these my brethren. . . ." Good heavens! You mean it was *you*? That time I just stopped by to see old Mrs. Thingummy? And that other time I didn't stop? But what sort of light does that throw on everything I do all day long?

A very frightening light. It seems to work both for good and ill. Edmund's disinclination to bother about Mr. Tumnus, small enough at the moment, is, alas, a deadly accurate index to what Edmund *is*: a selfish and egoistic cad. Emeth's service offered (he thought) to Tash is a deadly accurate index of what Emeth is: a good and right trusty servant. Digory's assumption that he has a right to try out anything (like ringing the little bell) is an accurate index to the character of a boy who lacks the modesty and hesitation that might protect him in the face of the perilous or the forbidden. A scuffle on the edge of a cliff, with Eustace trying to save Jill and then falling over—certainly not Jill's fault: but then, much later, it does seem, unhappily, that some sort of moral weight has been attached to those frantic and half-conscious motions in the struggle. Nothing at all seems to be neutral. It does not seem to matter much whether the incident was worth one talent or ten: the judgment is the same. Faithful custodianship of the small stuff qualifies one for bigger responsibilities. It seems to be true in more stories than one. Or put it another way: it becomes harder and harder to draw exact distinctions between fairy tales and "realistic" tales. Which elements do we wish to write off as implausible? Which oddities about the world of faerie are *not* true of ours?

This question of doing the thing that seems to present itself and that mere decency requires at the moment, appears

in an even starker light when it comes to clear duty. Again
and again in the chronicles we find someone faced with
some daunting task, and the thing which evaporates all theoretical protestings and dodgings, and which quite simply
requires the thing to be done, is duty. When Peter must
undergo his initiation on the way to being named High
King, and must kill the wolf, without any assistance from
Aslan (or so it appears), we have this: "Peter did not feel
very brave; indeed, he felt he was going to be sick. But
that made no difference to what he had to do." There seems
to be an implacable requirement laid upon everyone to do
the right thing, however small or big, at the moment when
it presents itself. No other principle will prove of much
assistance when the crunch comes. No uncertain emotions
will come to your aid then. No visions of glory which you
once saw will unfurl themselves and brace you. You've simply got to grit your teeth and do the impossible for no
other reason than that it is clearly the right thing to do.
Puddleglum is the great exemplar of this. It is not for nothing that Lewis has chosen this damp, gangling, gloomy,
unlikely, and ungainly marsh-dweller for his brightest hero
(even including Reepicheep): heroism does not mean *feeling* brave. There may be a few, a very few, plucky and blithe
spirits in the history of heroism who have *felt* like facing
the dragon or scaling the walls. But the rest of us, of whom
exactly the same tasks are asked, have got to get on with it
too. How in heaven and earth can ordeals like this be set
for us fainthearted types? The point is that they *are* set, and
the answer has something to do with plain training in obedience, which is itself an early lesson in the course which
leads us to discover that Aslan knew what he was doing all
along and knew exactly what was required to bring us to
the place where we could see and rejoice in and praise that

wisdom. But why is the language here getting theological? What we are talking about is fairy tales.

The center of gravity, so to speak, for the whole saga is of course Aslan. It seems to be important that he not appear very much. His comings and goings are infrequent, unpredictable and inexplicable. They follow no clearly observable pattern. It is worth noting that the very mention of his name has a certain effect. The Witch hates it. The first time the four children hear it the effect is as follows:

> *Edmund felt a sensation of mysterious horror. Peter felt suddenly brave and adventurous. Susan felt as if some delicious smell or some delightful strain of music had just floated by her. And Lucy got the feeling you have when you wake up in the morning and realize that it is the beginning of the holidays or the beginning of summer.*[2]

It seems that the name itself radiates sheer, searching truth, so that everything is naked and open before it.

There is a certain fear which attaches to the name of Aslan. It seems that he is the desire of every creature but also quite alarming—not at all a tame lion. Jill discovers this to her infinite dismay when she finds this threatening beast lying between her and the only water available to slake her thirst. Lewis comments:

> *People who have not been in Narnia sometimes think that a thing cannot be good and terrible at the same time. If the children had ever thought so, they were cured of it now. For when they tried to look at Aslan's face they just caught a glimpse of the golden mane and the great, royal, solemn,*

[2] C. S. Lewis, *The Lion, the Witch, and the Wardrobe* (New York: Collier Books, 1970), pp. 64, 65.

overwhelming eyes; and then they couldn't look at him and went all trembly.[3]

We find this paradox underscored in scene after scene throughout the chronicles; when we see Aslan surrounded by his loyal subjects, there is at once great solemnity and great joy. Susan and Lucy may romp with him and bury their faces in his mane after his reappearance from the dead: but one false step and the low rumble in his throat sounds the warning of forbidden borders about to be violated. And this same Aslan, the confidence and joy of his loyal subjects, is a terror and misery to the White Witches, Nikabriks, Uncle Andrews, and Rabadashes who run afoul of him.

News of Aslan and of his plans for Narnia seem to be found here and there in ancient rhymes and old lore, a motif that recurs in the chronicles. The great thing is to keep repeating the old formulas, and passing them down from generation to generation. The Beavers know the signs of the times from having been familiar with these old rhymes. Dr. Cornelius in *Prince Caspian* instructs the boy prince in the true history of his kingdom by telling him the old tales. In *The Silver Chair*, in an important variation on this theme, Aslan gives the children four things to remember, and their instructions are to keep saying these things over and over, to stamp them on their memories, to repeat them as they walk in the way, to bind them as frontlets between their eyes, and suddenly one finds that one has borrowed language from other ancient stories where the great thing was to remember what had been *said*, come hell or high water.

[3] Ibid., p. 123.

It is often by ordeal that each of the characters is tested in Narnia. The test is twofold as are all ordeals in fairy stories: first, to find out what a person is made of; and then to teach that person how to be something that he is not (brave or obedient or merciful or generous). Peter must fight his wolf, and Lucy must resist the temptations of the Magician's book, and Jill and Eustace must enter the very dwelling of the Green Witch, and Tirian must be lashed to a tree alone, and Digory must not eat the apple. But then we discover that there is a third, even more important point to the test: it always seems to be *for the sake of another*. There is no question of mere pointless testing, temptation, or suffering. In every case someone else's good is at stake. The frightening thing is that this good really does seem to depend on the response of the one being tested. There is the possibility of real loss (though not loss that cannot ultimately be repaired; for example, Edmund, forfeit to the Deep Magic from the Dawn of Time because of his greedy pusillanimity, was saved by the Deeper Magic from Before the Dawn of Time), but Aslan alone knows what price has to be paid for failure in the test.

This oddity—that real things really do depend on what seems to be the frailty of mere creatures (why doesn't Aslan just roar and have done with it?) also appears occasionally in a lighter context. At least four times in the battle in *The Lion, the Witch, and the Wardrobe* we see it. When they have finished the work of freeing the Witch's statues, they find themselves still locked in the courtyard of her castle. "Giant Rumblebuffin, just let us out of this, will you?" Aslan, who could have decimated the entire castle and all Narnia with it with one roar, calls upon the particular gift that giants bear and must use, namely sheer strength. Shortly after that, Aslan, in organizing the race to the scene of the battle, happens to say just in passing that those with good noses must come in front with "us lions". The other lion cannot get over it. "Did you hear what he said? *Us lions.* That means him and me. *Us lions.* That's what I like about Aslan. No side, no stand-offishness. *Us lions.* That means him and me." Somehow it is not according to the fabric that Narnia is made of that Aslan do it by fiat, alone. And then we see Peter and Edmund fighting as though the entire outcome depends on them, for as it happens it does, at that point. And finally, we see Lucy called upon to bring the phial of cordial, given her by Father Christmas, for the healing of the wounded. It must be she, and she must be quick about it.

Sooner or later, of course, it becomes impossible to carry the discussion of Narnia any further without finding ourselves quite unabashedly head over heels in the language of Christian vision and dogma: the Passion of Aslan; the Witch as Accuser of the brethren; the children made kings and queens; the "no need to talk" any more to Edmund of what is past since his transgressions have been blotted out as a thick cloud; the surly and egocentric nature of evil in Nikabrik, and the romantic megalomania in pitiable Uncle Andrew and in Jadis; the keeping of the "Hallows" (the Stone Knife) at Aslan's Table; the penitent star renewed day by day with a fire-berry brought from the Sun, and the discovery that what a star is *made of* does not tell the whole story of what a star *is*; the unbearable increase in the atmosphere's sweetness and clarity as the *Dawn Treader* nears the end of the world; the dryads and gnomes and salamanders and mermen who, like the skipping hills and singing morning stars of the Bible, populate the elements in the world that we nowadays see as mere "nature"; the awful sense in which various metamorphoses (Eustace's into a dragon, or Rabadash's into an ass) unveil what that person is; sheer, plain goodness (Frank the cabbie) as fitting one to see and hear splendors that the eyes and ears of egoism (Uncle Andrew) cannot perceive; the tree and the Garden, and the fruit "for others"; the rotten smell of Tash; the Stable whose inside is as big as the universe; and the final great rush up into joy—the joy that for us mortals here can only be pictured in this dazzling imagery of speed and laughter and reunion (especially the reappearance of Reepicheep) and of this *array* of creatures—unicorns, centaurs, dogs, and all—each bearing and exhibiting some unique aspect of the great Glory that flashes through the whole fabric.

Allegory is one way of pressing one thing into the service of another. But, despite many unmistakable, even exact, echoes in Narnia of what appears in our own story, and despite Professor Tolkien's objection that Lewis' Narnia chronicles are too woodenly allegorical, we may, it seems to me, see Lewis' achievement here, not so much in terms of allegory as of genuine fairy tale, which is what he meant to be writing. He tells us in his essay "Sometimes Fairy Stories May Say Best What's to Be Said" that he had fallen in love with the form of the fairy tale itself, "its brevity, its severe restraints on description, its flexible traditionalism, its inflexible hostility to all analysis, digression, reflections, and 'gas'. I was now enamoured of it. Its very limitations of vocabulary became an attraction; as the hardness of the stone pleases the sculptor or the difficulty of the sonnet delights the sonneteer."[4]

We may grant him his case, then: he wanted to write fairy tales. That we discover all sorts of elements in his tales that

---

[4] C. S. Lewis, *Of Other Worlds* (New York: Harcourt, Brace and World, 1966), p. 35.

stir us by their similarity to elements in our own story may be attributable to the same oddity that Merlin came upon when it seemed to him that Ransom was repeating an ancient druidical password which, it turns out, Ransom did not know about. "'But ... but ... if you knew not the password, how did you come to say it?' 'I said it because it was true.'"

CHAPTER THREE

Out of the Silent Planet: The Discarded Image

The first question we ask when we are presented with something new is, "What is it?" It may be a knucklebone of Saint Illtud or it may be a gimlet; but until we know what it is, we do not know how to react to it. Pushing this further, we do not know whether a thing is well made or shabbily made, beautiful or ugly, until we know what it is. If we suppose that a kite is made to carry great loads of freight we will conclude that it is too flimsy; or, conversely, if we think this coal-barge here is an entry in the America's Cup race, we will see it as a sorry piece of workmanship.

The same problem of definition, and of its corollaries beauty and excellence, obtains in all of the arts. A cathedral is full of wasted space, you can't whistle a tune in the *Well-Tempered Clavier*, and Rembrandt's paintings are all too dark; hence you will conclude that all of these are failures—unless you know what the thing is and therefore what the artist was aiming at.

The difficult question about the books in Lewis' space trilogy is, "What are they?" It is easy enough to locate the

Narnia tales. And *Till We Have Faces* may be put alongside
Ovid and Apuleius, if we wish, as a recent author's attempt
to come at ancient tales that were "in the air" long before
Lewis, Apuleius, or Ovid tried their hands at them. If we
balk at this then we may do with this trilogy what we do
with Tennyson's *Idylls of the King*, which we tend to put on
the Tennyson shelf: we may put it on the Lewis shelf. Reasonable enough, and who knows whether the Lewis shelf
may not become a fixity in libraries, even university libraries, before Western civilization has collapsed?

But that does not help us much with deciding what these
books are, and until that definition is reached, it is impossible to tell whether they are good.

That is the problem, set out in very theoretical terms.
But practically speaking there can be little doubt that the
element that stymies serious literary discussion of Lewis,
except among his votaries, is the element for which there
is no provision in the criticism of modern fiction, namely
the Ultimate.

There are some ironies at work here, of course. If the
criticism of modern fiction makes no provision for the
appearance of the Ultimate and therefore ignores most strictly
religious novels or tales of the occult, in what sense can we
maintain that Tolstoy or Dostoevsky do *not* write religious
novels? The whole point of Tolstoy's novella *The Death of
Ivan Ilych* is that release from the ghastly trap of his life
which *is* a death comes with the Orthodox sacrament of
forgiveness. What is that release? To what does it point? Or
in Kafka: by what literary canons are we permitted to suppose that a man can turn into a cockroach but not permitted to suppose that a man may meet an angel? Henry James
brings off *The Turn of the Screw* by leaving it very much in
doubt whether there is anything there at all (we are safe

with the psychological ambiguity of the terror involved). Or Flannery O'Connor: she is a serious contender for towering literary eminence, and she writes quite unabashedly about *God*. Indeed, she writes of nothing else. And not only God, but baptism and the Eucharist and grace and all sorts of other unmanageable and interdicted topics. François Mauriac, Graham Greene, Evelyn Waugh—they all brought their fiction to the threshold, indeed over the threshold, of this Ultimate. The mysteries bespoken in Catholic dogma furnish the dramatic center of gravity in half of the works of these writers.

What, then, qualifies and what does not? we may ask. If we may have the Mass, and a man turning into a cockroach, what mayn't we have? May we have revivalist novels about someone's getting *saved* and finding release from his dilemma the way Ivan Ilych was released?

And we find ourselves crowded along in the discussion to some such idea as this: you may have almost anything you want in your narrative. But you must show that the dramatic tension at work is really a tension that arises from recognizable, real human experience. You may not import into your tale forces or dramas that are not an acknowledged part of the immediate fabric of our lives. O'Neill may have a magic silver bullet, and Kafka a cockroach, and Beckett a God who won't arrive, but nonreligious men though we may be, we all find these images compelling. They speak accurately and powerfully of our real experience. They cast a stark light onto that experience. Very few of Tolstoy's readers are Orthodox: but who has not longed for some viaticum? Most of Flannery O'Connor's or Graham Greene's readers are not Catholics: but who of them cannot recognize the sort of pressure that sheer ultimacy imposes on us which these two writers choose to speak of under the imagery of, say, the Holy Ghost or the Mass? Flannery O'Connor, for example, ends one story with a water stain in the ceiling plaster above a sick young man's bed revealing itself to be, in effect, the Holy Ghost, brooding and descending like a bird on him. Her point, which we may take or leave, is that this is what the Holy Ghost does; ours might be that this is a vivid and fruitful metaphor for—for whatever we modern men suppose is there in place of the Holy Ghost. But everyone finds himself struck and riveted by the picture.

This brings us to Lewis, who regales us in *Out of the Silent Planet* with creatures like *hrossa* and *sorns* and *eldila*. Oh well then, Jules Verne and H. G. Wells and space fantasy. And yes, in a way—it is all that. But when we try to leave it at that we find that we have not even approached the substance of these tales. We have not, as Henry James would have us do, granted the writer his *donnée*, his starting point.

Like any worthy writer, Lewis has for his first concern the telling of a good story. Unless that is there, the whole enterprise is misbegotten. Lewis' own taste had always inclined him, no matter what else he may have been reading, to various kinds of adventure story. His letters contain references to his reading in Scott, Rider Haggard, and others, and not infrequently to writers of stories that entail the remote, the romantic, and even the magical: William Morris, Novalis, Maeterlinck, Grimm, and George MacDonald, especially MacDonald's fantasies.

So it is not surprising, for a start, to find Lewis' tales taking us off on sheer adventure. Fairy tales, interplanetary travel, King Arthur—all this, and more, is there. Couple this with Lewis' lifelong love for both Greek and Nordic myth, and his lifelong awareness of the longing that haunts all romantic imagination, and you have ingredients for tales that will stretch the category "realistic fiction", which is the category to which contemporary criticism commonly restricts itself.

But we may not leave it at that, for even though Lewis loved a good and unapologetic adventure story, adventure is not his central concern in his fiction. It is the *sine qua non* there, of course, as it must be for all narrative, at least in the sense of its entailing "an interesting story". In Lewis' case our interest is first roused by the business of interplanetary travel.

But we do not get very far in any of the tales, especially the space trilogy, before it becomes apparent that Lewis' interests cannot be said to be attaching to such mere matters as speed or danger or new scenery and strange creatures and all the rest of the "machinery" of space fantasy. Or put it another way: yes, the interest does attach to those things, but it attaches to them in the way Wordsworth's interest attaches to a vernal wood, or Spenser's to a grotto, or Coleridge's to the castle clock, or even Hopkins' to a darksome burn. It is, in other words, the *poet*'s interest, not the geographer's or the botanist's or the astrophysicist's. Or lest we be guilty of introducing a false distinction here, put it this way: poetry (that is, the literature of high imagination) carries the legitimate interest of all measurers and analysts (geographers, astrophysicists, all of us) on through to the clarity and intensity implicit in that interest from the outset. That is, if the botanist for example, finding himself galvanized by the efficiency and symmetry of the life forms he is scrutinizing, continues to press the questions implicit in notions like efficiency and symmetry, he is going to find himself reaching for such words as "beauty" and "pleasure" and "awe", and at this point he is going to need poetry, at least if he wants language to chart these latter developments in his study. It is not that poetry or the poetic imagination uncovers some arcane significance in things that a cloddish scientific analysis cannot hope to see: rather we may say that the poetic imagination wants to speak with a language that charts *how we mortals see* these phenomena, the thing implicit in poetry all along being that there is perhaps *no truer way to speak* of the phenomena.

Take, for example, Hopkins' "darksome burn": in a physics textbook this specimen of water seeking its own level might be adduced, and we might find a vocabulary of gravity, friction, wave motion, fluidity, and so forth, all of which would be true, useful, and interesting. What, then, is Hopkins speaking of with his "darksome burn, horseback brown / His roll-rock highroad roaring down" and so on? The maddening thing at work in all poetry is that this language speaks, not simply of our mortal feelings about the thing, but catches something which we are obliged to believe is true about it, and which will not yield to measurement and analysis. Whatever this quality is (the "reality" of the thing? the "truth" of the thing? the "mystery" of the thing?) will not be dismantled and measured: it can only be hailed or invoked, like a god.

And at this point we find ourselves in the language of mythology. Paradoxically it is our very attempt to keep our gaze fixed coldly, rigorously, and faithfully on the thing itself which has landed us here. We are after the truth of the darksome burn, not after feelings—at least it was not feelings we set out to capture. Even Wordsworth, perhaps the most shimmering of the poets on this front, is more curious about the power of the vernal wood to rouse certain feelings than he is about the nature of those feelings. The feelings may be tremulous or fugitive or blissful or powerful or ravaging or all five: but Wordsworth wants to know not so much how the feelings feel as what on earth it is about this wood that seems to release them. What intimation is here, what resident genius, what local deity? What footprint do we find left by what god? What tracks, what traces, what hints and guesses? We find that we confront an oddity that presented itself not only to Wordsworth and other "romantics" but also to Plato, Kant, Eliot, and, let us be candid, to every sage, seer, and poet. It is the problem of what is real, and of how we may hope to apprehend it, and of how it mediates itself to us, and of how we are to know whether we are talking merely of a bit of bad bacon that has given us dyspepsia and illusions, or whether this is heaven and hell looming upon us.

We have come here, it seems to me, to Lewis' central concern in *Out of the Silent Planet*. We cannot read far in this tale of interplanetary travel (which is sufficiently exciting in itself to have won the book a fairly steady place in the racks at airports and drug stores) without beginning to feel that there is far more at work in the action and the setting than mere intrigue, suspense, and interplanetary derring-do, although these are all there. This is not John Buchan. But it is not occult, or even necessarily "religious" either. The dramatic substance and force of the tale does not derive from the supposition that there are "powers" about. To be sure, the story supposes that there are; and, if we know something about Lewis' outlook on the world, we know that he also supposed this. But this supposition does not furnish us with the key to the literary worth of the tale, any more than the biological possibilities of a man's becoming a cockroach will give us a key to Kafka's achievement, or the efficacy of the Sacrament a key to Tolstoy's. Those elements are there, and they are crucial to the drama in the tales involved: but our agreement on Kafka's or Tolstoy's achievement in fiction will not depend upon our agreement over biological or sacramental questions. Similarly, the judgment that *Four Quartets* is one of the supreme poetic achievements of our epoch does not come only from Catholic Christians who might happen to share Eliot's theology. Somehow he has managed, not despite but by means of the vision and imagery at work in his poem, to do undeniable justice to human experience. This notion of the redemption of time (which Eliot, being Christian, really did espouse) is more than convenient or useful or suggestive: it is *true*. He has touched exquisitely on the central nerve of our existence. Even the critic who may himself be a materialist will agree. Eliot's is a true, not a false, vision.

We do not, in other words, write off a story or a poem because it supposes ideas which are no longer taken seriously by Western man. On that accounting we will have to write off everyone from Homer to Tolstoy. If we agree upon this, however, we may not thereby conclude that a writer's achievement is of the first rank *because* his tale shares suppositions with Homer and Dante, say. On that accounting Superman and Donald Duck suddenly take their places beside Zeus and Beatrice by exhibiting no other virtue than that of being "nonrealistic".

Our inquiry into Lewis' achievement in his space trilogy, and specifically in *Out of the Silent Planet*, must pursue questions such as what his central concern is, and whether that concern is an important one, and then how well he did, on purely artistic grounds, in dramatizing that concern.

What, then, is Lewis' concern in this tale? There is a revealing exchange in the very last chapter. Ransom, the protagonist, has returned from his voyage to Malacandra (the planet we would call Mars). His experience there has been ecstatic and awesome beyond hope or imagination. The natural thing will be to tell the world about it. But he abandons the idea, for a simple, twofold reason: first, he finds that he himself wonders how much of it all may have been delusion, knowing full well that there are ready psychoanalytic explanations for everything he thinks he saw. Second, who will believe it?

But then in conversation with Lewis (who is in the story as narrator the way Conrad allows himself or his narrator Marlow to preside over a story at one remove from the action), Ransom comes to see that though no one will credit a syllable of the story as scientific truth, yet it might be worth telling—nay, it must be told—*as fiction*. "What we need for the moment is not so much a body of belief as a body of people familiarized with certain ideas."

Here we have Lewis' whole fictional concern in a nutshell. Here is what animates his narrative art. It is as though he says to himself and thence to us, "We have stories aplenty these days of this, that, and the other. Good stuff. Now: may we have stories once more (they used to be told) of something altogether *other*? Is it possible to tell tales that will carry us into vistas of terror and joy that have gone quite out of our ken in recent centuries? Not, pray understand, by way of siphoning our attention away from a gritty reality that has become intolerable in our century as a sort of opiate, but quite to the contrary, by way of shaking us all awake from the poisonous torpor that settled over human imagination a few centuries ago."

Or put it this way: what imagery shall we find that will do justice to much that seems implicit in our experience of existence but that never seems to find a correlative objective enough to hold it? May we at least attempt to clarify and harden into an image the thing which most certainly haunts all of our experience here—the thing for which he can find no name since it exists only by being implicit or inchoate in our experience? We call it Beauty or Perfection or Joy or even Paradise; and its obverse side is Horror and Chaos and Doom and Vacuity and even Hell. Shall this not be stuff for modern fiction? If not, why not? Have we established finally that it is forever irrelevant or misleading or trivial? The myths may speak of it, and Homer and Dante and Hopkins and Eliot. Is the writer of fiction disqualified? Must we assign this sort of thing to "peculiar" categories—the sort of categories that exist for Hakluyt's travels, and Gulliver, and *Alice in Wonderland*?

In *Out of the Silent Planet* Lewis is a storyteller, not a critic, so he does not so much argue the answer, or even ask the theoretical question, as simply wade into the business of trying his hand at a tale of this sort.

The "certain ideas" mentioned by Ransom may be focused in one central idea which he articulates thus: "If we could even effect in one percent of our readers a change-over from the conception of Space to the conception of Heaven, we should have made a beginning."

That mild hope of course points to a Himalayan watershed running across human imagination. Is the universe to be imagined under an imagery of distance and mechanics, or of dance and solemnity and joy? The question is not just a cosmological one, however: the way we conceive it shapes our imagination entirely and hence determines our art. Do we incline to paint Annunciations or soup tins? Shall we have Zeus Pater or a parking meter for our sculpture? May we speak of the Celestial Rose in our poetry as well as of the smells of steaks in passageways?

Lewis' own answer to these questions is no secret, and he spelled out many of the attendant concerns in both *The Discarded Image* and *The Abolition of Man*.

Out of the Silent Planet is the lightest of Lewis' narratives. The nature of his achievement here will not be found by looking for dense dramatic complexity, nor for subtleties in human situations, those well-proved components of the modern novel. Rather, we will discover what he is about only by doing what we do with any narrative or drama, namely by watching closely what the artist is up to and forming our impressions accordingly.

The action unfolds in a plain linear way, the way the action does in most adventure stories. We find a university don off on his walking holiday alone in the English countryside, looking for a night's lodging at a farm. Complications arise in an entirely plausible way, and before we know where we are, we are away from Earth altogether, en route to a planet. So far all is fairly straightforward.

But if we will attend to how the narrator is giving us his account of this adventure, we will find that there are some suppositions at work that at first seem so obvious as to be unnoticeable, but that gradually emerge, like the dawn, as the thing which separates night from day, or evil from good: in other words, as the dramatic center of gravity. Here is how it first emerges. The don, whose name is Ransom, has quite by chance stumbled upon a woman who is frantic with worry about her son Harry who has not come home from work. (It seems that the boy works as a handyman for a professor who keeps a cottage nearby.) Ransom has no natural interest in this diversion: he is looking for lodging and would like to get on with it. Well then, "It occurred to [Ransom] that he ought to call on the mysterious professor", and presently this rather small, parenthetical decision "had assumed all the solidity of a thing determined upon."

So he goes. Surely the action has not got into full swing yet? Well no, not the interplanetary excitement to be sure.

But that interplanetary excitement turns out to be, like Macbeth's or Lear's or Othello's situations, the dramatic setting for what is at work anyway, all the time, in Lear's life, or Macbeth's, or Ransom's, or yours or mine or Adam's, and that tends not to be noticed until it is blazoned on some great banner that we call a "dramatic" situation, either on stage or, unhappily, in our actual experience. Presumably all murders, for example, are "merely" the dramatic unfolding of energetic evils that are at work in all of us a good bit of the time; the curtain does not usually go up on anything as stark as a murder for us because we manage to keep it down by resorting to "mini-murders" like snubs or insults or frosty cordiality or sulking—all ways of striking back at someone who has, we think, done us wrong.

The thing which just barely begins to appear here with Ransom is this: Ransom's present situation, and his inclination, and his convenience, and his wish for a lodging, and every other personal interest, would urge him most strongly to avoid any sort of entanglement with this nervous old woman. After all, she is just a frantic old thing, and the boy will certainly be along any moment, and what I want and need is a place to lodge, and it will set my schedule back by who knows how much time if I get waylaid here.

Quite correct, Ransom. Your analysis is probably accurate in every detail. What is it, then, that overrides these vastly plausible arguments, and lands Ransom in the very thing that makes very little sense if what he is after is rest after his day's tramping? Two things: first, his plain, stock, traditional, schoolboy, civilized training in decency. It has nothing in the world to do with how he *feels*, and worse, nothing in the world to do with his convenience. There it is, like the Great Wall of China, running right across the landscape of a man's life, with civility and helpfulness and courtesy and decency (*and* inconvenience and irritating responsibilities and wasted time) on the inside; and barbarianism and selfishness and egoism and cutting into lines (*and* convenience snatched from others' pockets, and boring situations avoided, and all sorts of unpaid-for delights) on the outside. Call it bourgeois morality, or middle-class values, or the Boy Scouts or society's stereotypes or conventional behavior, or whatever we want: the thing undergirding it is the thing undergirding all possibility of civil human life, namely the recognition of the prior claim that the other person has on your own claim to yourself. Nonsense, madness, and irritation—but this frenzied old woman here has a claim on me as absolute and serene as if she were the empress of all the Russias. Damn and blast.

But there it is. It is what your nanny and your mother and your father and your schoolmasters taught you: let *him* go first! pass it to her first! wait till the others have been served! stand up! hush! smile! shake hands! Oh damn, damn, damn! Why won't they leave me alone?

They won't leave you alone, boy, because left thus alone you would turn into a cad and thence into a monster and thence into a damned soul. That is the long and the short of it, and it is the watershed between what Lewis (along with all Hebrew prophets and Greek sages and all lawgivers and saints in all societies) conceived of as the very pattern of authentic human life and the very guardian of liberty and joy—between that on the one hand and the notion presiding over all modern views of human behavior, namely that it is self-assertion and freedom from restraint that will bring us to our true stature and wholeness.

But this is to get, or at least to seem to get, too far afield from Ransom and the old woman. The point is that it is not so very far afield. All this and more is very much at work in that one sentence fragment in the narrator's account, "It occurred to him that he ought to call on the mysterious professor. . . ." *Ought.* It engaged the mind of Immanuel Kant himself. The Great Wall. Inside and outside. Civility and barbarity. Joy or wrath. Paradise or perdition. The City of God or hell. The end point of all dramas and all art.

But it would seem also to be departing altogether from the business of literary criticism to set sail on a moral and philosophical sea like this on the strength of one word. Can an author not use one word without our seizing upon it with "Aha! There you have it!" and proceeding to write our own homily upon the text? Can Henry James never use the word "bore" without our offering a disquisition upon Ultimate Ennui, or D. H. Lawrence never say "blood" without the whole history of propitiation being invoked? Well, yes, of course: *unless* those one-syllable words happen to name the business that the author is dramatizing. (In neither of the examples from James or Lawrence would it seem that any such thing is in fact at work.) When we come upon the word "wrath" in Homer, that one word may carry a gigantic and significant freight.

So Ransom turns aside. But there is amelioration. And here is the second thing which moves Ransom to this course of action. It is not all sheer, gritty duty and nobility. It also "occurs" to him that, by calling on the professor, he just might find the hospitality he seeks for the night. In the sort of world we find in Lewis' narratives these moral cruxes seldom come to us stark and unvarnished with "Here's your duty and it's all unselfishness" pitted against "There's your own interest and that's all pleasure." Often it is slightly muddled. Some amelioration may sweeten the duty. As often as not a man may discover that sheer duty happens to include pleasures or conveniences that he might otherwise miss. We do not often, in the course of one lifetime, witness a full-dress Gethsemane. We may, but it will have been our responses in earlier situations, helped by small ameliorations, that will equip us to face the duty that is unsweetened by any amelioration at all.

There is one other straw in the dramatic wind in this small scene. The old woman's situation and the possibility of lodging work briefly in Ransom's mind, and he decides to go and see about her son. But this decision did not form itself in his conscious process of thought, weighing this and that, arriving at a clear juncture, and then girding up his moral loins and making the jump—the decision to help her. Rather, "whatever the process of thought may have been, he found that the mental picture of himself calling at The Rise [the professor's cottage] had assumed all the solidity of a thing determined upon." "Mental picture . . . solidity". The moral thing came to him eventually as an imaginative thing. It was not so much a matter of coping with abstract moral conundrums, and of quickly trying to sort through the whole process of pro and con, which would have mired him in an ethical bog like Hamlet, as it was a matter of finding that the picture of himself *doing* it had come before his eyes. Psychologically speaking we may maintain of course that this picture did, in fact, follow upon a very swift and mostly unconscious mental process. Fine. But it is the *picture* which is the operative thing in moving him to action.

And not only that. It assumes this solidity—"the solidity of a thing determined upon". This is at work throughout the fabric of Lewis' narratives, because it is in the fabric of the universe (he would say). Somewhere in our moral ponderings things solidify—for good or ill. We do not have the option of hesitating forever. Somehow, while the question

is still open we find that we have taken action—or refused
to do so. To opt for some course of action is not to have
laid to rest every objection to it, nor to have silenced every
possible caution or qualification. Of course (says the World
War I subaltern in the trench) if I leap over the top here I
shall be shot. But here I go. What makes him do it? Titanic
heroism? Mere training in obeying orders? That it is the
next thing to do? That everyone else is also going over? All
these and no doubt more are all mixed in somehow; but
the difference between the man who goes over the top and
the one who collapses whimpering in the bottom of the
trench is not how they feel (they both feel the same way),
nor is it a matter of the one's having reached a clear and
rational point of view on the pros and cons of going over
and of the other's having been unable to do so. The man
going over is, as it were, an actor in his own picture of a
man going over: here's how a man going over looks—
clamber up here—leg up—other one—NOW!

In many of Lewis' narratives we find this solidifying at
work. Somehow tendencies and habits and inclinations suddenly (or gradually: but you never know at what point they
are no longer pliable or malleable) solidify, and there you
are, stuck with the image you've made. A querulous little
boy left to his own inclinations may become the very image
of pusillanimous tyranny. A boy who now and again covers
his tracks with minor juggling of the truth may, unless something like a parent or a teacher cuts across this habit, become
a monster of falsehood. A boy pulling the legs off flies may
become an inquisitor unless some lessons in mercy inter-
vene. If this seems extreme and alarmist, we may rake through
the biographies of every saint and tyrant in history: what
did they look like as mere boys? What nudged them in the
direction they finally took? Uncle Andrew—Rabadash—

Weston—Wither—how did they get that way? Eustace—Edmund—Jane—Mark—Orual—what rescued them?

The solidifying is both a major and a long-range business, in which a man reaps in his character the fruit of small habits and attitudes, and also the business of a moment in which action supplants pondering. At some point Ransom must stop hesitating and set out for the professor's cottage.

We find this business of a man's being governed by the conventions of decency rather than selfishness spelled out in *The Abolition of Man* and *A Preface to Paradise Lost* in Lewis' discussions of "stock responses". By this phrase he refers to those ways of reacting in situations that mark us as civilized men but that we have had to acquire, since they do not come naturally to us. With most of his heroes—Peter, Puddleglum, Ransom, even Orual—the good or brave act is supported almost solely by a sense of "Well, there's nothing for it now but to *do* it. Heaven knows I'm terrified (or irritated), and no doubt I will fail. But there is no question of *not* doing it." This sense always seems to be one that has been acquired from training in conventional behavior, having nothing whatever to do with one's feelings.

When, later in this narrative, we find Ransom ready to collapse upon discovering that he is in a spaceship heading away from earth, we find that he wishes that death or sleep, or best of all waking from this dream, might come to his rescue. Nothing comes. "Instead, the lifelong self-control of social man, the virtues which are half hypocrisy or the hypocrisy which is half a virtue, came back to him...."

A variation on this theme arises when, much later, Ransom in Malacandra must make the journey to Meldilorn where the Oyarsa dwells, although there are various reasons for perhaps not going.

> *He made a strong resolution, defying in advance all changes*
> *of mood, that he would faithfully carry out the journey to*
> *Meldilorn if it could be done. This resolution seemed to him*
> *all the more certainly right because he had the deepest mis-*
> *givings about that journey.*[1]

In other words, Ransom knows enough to realize that when
action is necessary, it must be supported by something more
solid than inclination, since mere inclination will be wafted
quite away at the first puff of adversity. In the "temptation"
scene that follows immediately, when various misgivings and
plausibilities arise to deflect Ransom from his task, he keeps
going, and thinks back on his first day here in Malacandra:
"Then all had been whimpering, unanalyzed, self-nourishing,
self-consuming dismay. Now, in the clear light of an accepted
duty, he felt fear indeed, but with it a sober sense of confidence. . . ."[2]

We may also note that when Ransom approaches the cottage of the professor, having promised the old woman that
he would at least have a look, all sorts of reasons present
themselves to him for not going through with it. "He did
not want to. A nice fool he would look, blundering in upon
some retired eccentric ... with this silly story of a hyster-
ical mother in tears"[3] and so on. But he must do it, and,
in order to get through the hedge (the gate is locked) he
flings his pack over the gate. "The moment he had done
so, it seemed to him that he had not till now fully made up
his mind—now that he must break into the garden if only
in order to recover the pack." Once more we find that the

[1] C. S. Lewis, *Out of the Silent Planet* (New York: Macmillan Publishing Company, 1965), p. 85.

[2] Ibid., p. 86.

[3] Ibid., p. 10.

big duty is "mediated" to a man by being broken down into smaller, more manageable bits, and that sheer resolve is assisted by the necessity of small, more proximate steps. Ransom is helped over a literal and metaphorical hurdle (the hedge) not by any stout resolve to be charitable and brave and help the old woman, but, at the point itself, by the very marginal business of retrieving his pack—the pack which he flung over, again not in any great act of pluck but simply because you can't get through a hedge very well with a pack on your back. Down, down, down it all comes: the big moral issues mediating themselves in very small, very manageable bits. Assaulting the gates of hell would daunt the most blithe and heroic spirit; but it probably comes down to struggling with this ladder here, and putting my shoulder to the wheel of this battering ram that is stuck in the mud here, and getting past this gorse thicket, and so forth. The heroic ordeal known as Assaulting the Gates of Hell would be too daunting, and I would quail. But I can at least get this wretched ladder to stand straight . . .

If it seems a prolonged and laborious business to scrutinize the events this narrowly, we may recall two things: first, when you are speaking of *how* a given poet or storyteller goes about his work, you find that a certain amount of squinting is necessary. It is all very well to point out how easy it is to tell a Spenser line from a Wordsworth line. But beyond giving examples, can we *say* what that difference is? In order to do this, we must get down to close work. It is even more difficult with prose. We may rake up paragraphs from Jane Austen and Thomas Hardy that will exhibit great differences in style: but to explain how the two novelists go about their writing, and how this procedure shows up in the fabric of their work—that is a matter of rigorous, even myopic, scrutiny.

Second, we may recall that Lewis is attempting something in narrative for which he had few if any precedents. It is not just psychological realism that he is attempting—that patient and subtle charting of the very contours of experience as it comes to us daily, which forms the substance of the modern novel; nor is it mere escape and thrill, which accounts for the mass of space fiction, murder mystery, romance, and adventure that makes up the huge majority of prose fiction. Nor is it religious or allegorical or moral fiction, where the writer attempts to smuggle into our consciousness some improving thoughts or prophetic insights. Of course any fiction probably contains elements of all three, in the sense that any writer wants to make his characters seem real and wants to keep us reading, and if he is serious about his art, wants to make us see life in a certain light. But Lewis is attempting to arrange the elements in his story— the setting and the events and the characters and the narrative technique itself—so that we will see not another world but our own existence and our own experience as it may appear when seen from such and such an angle—that angle being not some private vision of Lewis' but the angle from which Greek, Jew, and Christian vision have seen it for some millennia. In other words, Lewis is attempting to achieve in prose narrative what has been attempted in epic or dream vision or religious lyric in other eras of literature, namely the placing of human experience in the bright light of the Ultimate. The important questions at work in this light are not so much social and psychological as moral. Behavior is good or bad, and it leads to actual states of being, those states being called, eventually, heaven and hell. This is imagined in Greek epic and in the myths and in mediaeval dream vision and in the poetry of such poets as Spenser, Milton, Donne, and Eliot. It is not common in prose fiction.

We may now observe the forward movement of Lewis' narrative, noting how he drives the action along and what elements he chooses to emphasize. These may furnish us with some ability to reach generalizations as to the nature of his craft, which is, after all, what criticism should be doing.

We may note, for example, that the whole question of technology is of no importance whatever in this narrative, which is an oddity in "space fiction". With the barest minimum of comment, the spaceship leaves Earth, travels, and arrives in Malacandra. Problems of propulsion and atmosphere and so forth are subsumed under larger concerns. An author has this privilege: Shakespeare is not obliged to settle pneumatological questions before sending a ghost onto the stage in *Hamlet*.

We may note also, as we must in any fiction, how the author handles the business of character. In an allegory like *Pilgrim's Progress*, for example, you may find two-dimensional characters, like the characters in the morality plays and the masques who said in so many words, "I am Pride", or, "I am Everyman." That is one sort of character treatment. At the other pole you find Anna Karenina or Jude (the obscure one, not the epistoler), who are fully developed people whom we get to know intimately in all of their ambiguity, suffering, and complexity. This latter sort of portraiture is, surely, the great achievement of the modern novel. No other art form has caught quite this angle on the way in which the bits of our day-to-day experience constitute the mosaic which, seen from a distance, turns out to be Human Experience.

It is difficult to find convenient categories in which to classify Lewis' handling of character. If we think of the two-dimensional characters of allegory as painted in bold and simple primary colors, say, and of the fully developed characters of the great novels as painted with subtle color and intricate brushwork, it will become apparent that the characters whom we meet in Lewis' fiction do not fit either group. In *Out of the Silent Planet* what do we find? There are only two principal characters—Ransom and Weston. And it does not take us long to discover that this is anything but a novel of "character". To urge that it is, and to try to wring from this story what we can wring from the stories of Anna or Jude, would be to ignore the most obvious elements of the tale, namely the elaborately and painstakingly depicted landscape of Malacandra, the presence of the other creatures in Malacandra, and the nature of the conflict that arises in the action. We are always obliged to pay attention to all that a dramatist or storyteller is doing; it is no good complaining that Romeo is not as fully developed as Hamlet, or that Theseus is much less interesting than Prospero. That would be to ignore nearly everything that Shakespeare is up to.

We learn a good deal about Ransom in this first scene: he is a philologist, which will turn out to be increasingly significant as the trilogy progresses, since language itself touches on some of the central points of interest. And he is obviously a decent and plain man with what seem to be routinely generous instincts. He is far from being an adventurer: his solitary walk with his map and his pack is his ideal holiday. And he is far from being impressive. When he accosts the two men struggling with the boy, instead of thundering out some imprecation, all he can manage is a singularly *un*impressive "Here! I say!"

The next person we meet is Devine, whom we will also see diabolically transfigured in *That Hideous Strength*. So far he is only a cad and a bore. Ransom had known him at school, and at that school,

Devine had learned just half a term earlier than anyone else that kind of humor which consists in a perpetual parody of the sentimental or idealistic clichés of one's elders. For a few weeks his references to the Dear Old Place and to Playing the Game, to the White Man's Burden and a Straight Bat, had swept everyone, Ransom included, off their feet.[4]

Later Ransom had wondered "how anyone so flashy and, as it were, ready-made, could be so successful."

This sort of hearty, slightly bullying, but eminently natural, schoolboy cleverness is both common and understandable. The difficulty is that it contains the ingredients of damnation. The destruction of sentiment (proper sentiment— the sort of thing at work, say, in *dulce et decorum est pro patria mori*) clears the way for pure cynicism which leads to brutishness. This can be traced in any society which becomes clever, sophisticated, and finally blasé. The next thing you get is a donnybrook. Lewis argued all this in *The Abolition of Man*, and it forms, of course, one of the central concerns in *That Hideous Strength*. So far we have it only in glimpses of Devine. We cannot pretend that Devine is more than a sketchy character, but then everyone but the two or three central characters in any drama is sketchy. Otherwise you have a mob on stage. Shakespeare cannot make Alonzo or Trinculo as large and colorful as Prospero.

Weston is another matter. He is a major figure in both *Out of the Silent Planet* and *Perelandra*. But he is developed with only the sparest of lines. We first see him struggle with the recalcitrant boy, trying as it turns out to bundle him into the space vehicle to be taken to Malacandra as a sacrifice. There, in a nutshell, is the whole of Weston. In

[4] Ibid., p. 15.

the flat-out pursuit of his gigantic vision of a scientific utopia, not only for our world but for all worlds, he has extinguished in himself every rag of plain, normal, traditional
human generosity and charity. Damn the boy: he's worthless
anyway, and his sacrifice is in the interest of the secular paradise we are organizing. Weston speaks the language of all
secular utopians of the Right or the Left, where you find
the ideal being invoked to justify every sort of meddlesome-
ness, cruelty, and tyranny. It does not much matter to the
plain citizen whether the vision at the top is Nazi, Bolshe-
vik, or Liberationist: what he finds is that slogans and fierce
programs designed to bring about some huge common good
progress from meddlesome legislation to tumescent bureau-
cracy to repression to inquisition to slaughter. The twentieth century has chosen to limit its awareness of spectacles
like this to Nazi Germany. It has been less willing to see the
same thing at work in Leninist and Stalinist Russia or Mao's
China, and altogether unwilling to see intimations of the
same thing in the sagging bureaucracies of liberal democracy. (Lewis, by the way, was a democrat, and spoke more
than once to this point. It is pure ignorance of his work that
leads some of his critics to accuse him of being a sort of
absolute monarchist. He was aware of certain values that gather
and are preserved in the imagery of crowned heads; but he
was also aware enough of human cupidity to fear any sort of
government that entrusted power to few hands. What he
distrusted in our own massively democratic era was the murderous pettiness of bureaucrats, and the brutalizing effect of
a society that has been "planned" according to modern scientific definitions of what humanness really is.)

The frightening thing about Weston is that what begins
modestly enough as a mixture of a testy personality, single-
minded devotion to an idea, and an effort to be completely

objective ends up in a state that can be depicted only under the imagery of damnation. Nothing less will quite do the trick. In the interest of "realism", Lewis might have chosen some milder apotheosis for Weston; but that would be to have written a different story. To ask him to have done so would be analogous to asking Henry James to leave out, in the interest of credibility, the difficult notion of the preternatural in *The Turn of the Screw*, or Shakespeare to have spared us Banquo's ghost.

We are given intimations of the apocalyptic moral magnitude of Weston's notions when we hear him saying such things as this:

> . . . *small claims must give way to great. As far as we know, we are doing what has never been done in the history of man, perhaps never in the history of the universe. We have learned how to jump off the speck of matter on which our species began; infinity, and therefore perhaps eternity, is being put into the hands of the human race. You cannot be so small-minded as to think that the rights or the life of an individual or of a million individuals are of the slightest importance in comparison with this.* [5]

There are old names in literature for that sort of thing. It has been known for some millennia as *hubris*, or ambition, or overweening pride; and it is what brought down Lucifer and Adam and Phaeton and Daedalus and Macbeth and the rest of us.

Weston's assumption is that his point of view is right at least partly because is it what is happening. It is the "next thing", and in the mythology of progress this next thing is,

---

[5] Ibid., p. 27.

by definition, a good thing. It is inevitable. (What happens, in this view, with prophetic warnings such as one might direct to someone who was speeding off a cliff, is not clear.) And the agent and mediator of this progress, on Weston's view, is science. "... All educated opinion—for I do not call classics and history and such trash education—is entirely on my side", says Weston.[6] Here again the common notion that Lewis is antiscience springs from plain ignorance. Over and over he rings the changes on the thing that he fears, and it is not science itself. After all, science is a certain method of inquiry into certain kinds of data. It is neutral, like economics or psychology or literary criticism. What Lewis fears is scientific materialism raised to a philosophy and imposed on society and morals.

There is, however, an irony at work in Weston's scientific pretensions. Oddly, it is the ivory-tower Ransom who finds himself more naturally at home in the strange terrain of Malacandra than the scientist Weston, who ought, by any common reckoning, to be the one prepared to accommodate himself to new data and new terrain. In so small a detail as lunch when they arrive in Malacandra, we may see this: Ransom notices that the water they drink is taken from the water-tins which Weston has brought, and not from the blue lakes. Weston's assumption is that this is terrain to be conquered, not enjoyed. He has no interest whatever in the possibility that these lovely lakes might supply water of a clarity and sweetness beyond earthly capacity to imagine. Sweetness indeed! Another of your sentimental categories. This whole realm is obviously hostile.

This attitude, harmless enough on this level, becomes murderous in Weston's assumption that insofar as a creature is

---

[6] Ibid.

alien it is hostile. This is a common assumption in a great deal of space fiction, from H. G. Wells on down. But what is the seed of this supposition? Might it be some egotistical chauvinism on our part that sees all other selves as probably ignorant and certainly less fortunate than we? Or is it perhaps some inability to see other creatures as selves at all, and to see them only as data, or worse, hostile data? In any event, Weston quite casually kills one of the creatures native to Malacandra, a *hross*, as a hunter in our world would shoot a gopher. The grim thing is that Ransom has met these *hrossa*, and they turn out to be an exquisitely graceful, even lyrical, species of creature, who seem to embody in the common routines of their lives all that we earthbound mortals ordinarily attach to the highest notions of "poet".

This murderous myopia on Weston's part—after all, he has spent his adult life squinting closely at data, so myopia of spirit is an appropriate characteristic—comes to a ghastly and comic fruition at the Malacandrian consistory, or tribunal, where, quite blind to the starkly clear and solemn outlines of the larger situation surrounding him, Weston gibbers on to the assembled creatures (he sees them the way pith-helmeted Englishmen saw the Hottentots) in pidgin English, threatening them with his "puff-bang" and finally attempting to divert them by dangling beads in front of them and dancing an ungainly pirouette. The serene majesty before whom he has been haled, and the serried ranks of beauty that form the court—data like this have never shown up in his lenses and test tubes, so of course he has no way of seeing them at all. It is a theme that we encounter more than once in Lewis—the idea of the *inanity* of evil. Lewis did not make up the idea: there is at least Dante's "loss of the good of intellect" for precedent. (Devine, it may be noticed, seems to be limited to plain, imbecile, infantile greed so far: he wants only the "sun's blood"—gold—that Malacandra offers. His damnation is not even *interesting*: hell is a bore, among other things. Fathomless ennui, forever and ever.)

But to treat Lewis' fiction as though character portrayal, at least as we usually think of it in fiction, is the central concern would be akin to treating Beethoven's symphonies as though they were demonstrations of cello technique: that may be part of the story but it can hardly be urged that it exhausts the account of what is going on. It is to ignore other elements that constitute major components in the design.

One does not read far in this narrative without realizing that page after page is being spent in nothing more than the description of scenery, and of Ransom's feelings upon encountering this scenery. We first come upon this during the voyage to Malacandra. As Ransom comes to his senses in the spaceship after having been drugged and shanghaied, he finds himself "poised on a sort of emotional watershed from which, he felt, he might at any moment pass into delirious terror or into an ecstasy of joy." [7] What is happening, of course, in Lewis' mythic cosmography, is that Ransom is going *in*. In to Deep Heaven, in to the Field of Arbol (what we, shut on the silent planet Thulcandra, call, with metallic dullness, the solar *system*). Far from finding that everything is getting thinner and colder and more vacuous, Ransom discovers what can perhaps only be called a *weight* of glory. Beauty surrounds them, dances before them, presses upon them, thickens and hardens until it is unbearable. We find this sort of vocabulary:

> . . . *the tyranny of heat and light* . . . *the palest of all imaginable golds* . . . *intense alacrity* . . . *he felt vigilant, courageous and magnanimous* . . . *stars, thick as daisies* . . . *planets*

[7] Ibid., p. 23.

of unbelievable majesty . . . celestial sapphires. . . . The adven-
ture was too high, its circumstance too solemn, for any emo-
tion save a severe delight . . . unrelenting though unwounding
brightness . . . depth after depth of tranquillity.[8]

This is the language of ecstatic sanctity—the sort of thing
we might encounter in Isaiah, Saint John the Divine, and
Saint Teresa. And of course this is the point. Perhaps the
image, discarded by the world now, of the universe as a
solemn and rapturous Dance, and of that glory being the
unfurling in gigantic colors of what appears in the human
spirit as virtue, and all of it, small and great, being the very
diagram of Charity, which speeds from the Center, flashing
through every motion of the Dance and suffusing the whole
with joy—perhaps that image may be useful in a piece of
fiction by way of experiment. Let us try it out, Lewis seems
to suggest in his fiction. Let us see if this imagery does any
sort of justice to our experience. May we mortals be permitted to imagine what is perhaps implicit in all the hints
and guesses that press upon us from our experience every
day all day all our lives long, and that have animated poets
and bards for millennia? If we find that it all falsifies our
experience or trivializes it, or beckons us away from that
experience, or merely throws gold dust in our eyes so that
we can no longer see the outlines of that experience with
accuracy—if this is the net effect of this sort of fiction, then
of course we must disavow it. For fiction should have for
its purpose, says Conrad, the rendering of the "highest possible justice" to the stuff of our experience, at least if we
are to regard it as a worthy thing.

The real question at work here is whether you can make
fiction out of all this. To what extent is the artist obliged to

[8] Ibid., pp. 29–31.

limit himself to the vision of things at work in his own era? Can he paint Annunciations or fauns? At least part of the dramatic force at work in Lewis' fiction is this very sort of question pressing on a very contemporary and ordinary man, Dr. Elwin Ransom. If *we* wonder about it, so does he. En route to Malacandra "he found it night by night more difficult to disbelieve in old astrology: almost he felt, wholly he imagined, 'sweet influence' pouring or even stabbing into his surrendered body."[9] Where Weston, the doctrinaire scientific materialist, refers to all this bliss as "rays" that never reach us down on earth, Ransom's experience must be described thus:

> *A nightmare, long engendered in the modern mind by the mythology that follows in the wake of science, was falling off him. He had read of "Space": at the back of his thinking for years had lurked the dismal fancy of the black, cold vacuity, the utter deadness, which was supposed to separate worlds. He had not known how much it affected him till now—now that the very name "Space" seemed a blasphemous libel for this empyrean ocean of radiance in which they swam. . . . No: Space was the wrong name. Older thinkers had been wiser when they named it simply the heavens—the heavens which declared the glory.*[10]

The Wellsian fantasy of a universe "peopled with horrors" is, perhaps, not the only way of fancying it all.

This is to imply that the proper place for Lewis' work is on the shelf next to Wells, since they at least both wrote about space travel. That may be as much as we can hope

[9] Ibid., p. 31.
[10] Ibid., p. 32.

from the literary judgment of our own era. But two things at least must be included in that judgment: the whole "feel" of Lewis' work in fiction is remote from anything that Wells was interested in; and, more important, the whole set of interests that animates Lewis' fiction is very far indeed from what we find in Wells. If we want to locate Lewis' work with respect to these interests, we would have to find a space somewhere near Dante and Eliot. (This is with reference to interests alone: we are not speaking of achievement here.)

Lewis' fiction in this regard does bring us near the lodestar that seems, oddly, to drag all human inquiry and imagination toward itself, namely the point at which everything that rises converges. It was easy enough to tuck things into the "mythic" category when, say, one hundred years ago it was supposed that science could tell us the clear truth. But then you press astrophysics far enough and you are darting about amongst black holes that look for all the world like apertures into other dimensions of being that we have no way of measuring and that we can speak of only in the language hitherto reserved for myth or fantasy. And of course mathematicians for centuries have had to reach for the language of beauty to describe what it is they perceive in the higher reaches of their inquiries. The astronauts, those very icons of modern technology, must hold their breath with awe at the majesty of what they see.

The point here is not to suggest that perhaps, if we travel far enough, we will see the Field of Arbol from the window, but rather that what we are speaking of is something imaginative at work in Lewis' fiction: not imaginative in the sense that his setting is speculative (though it is), but rather in the sense that the whole drama—action, character, setting, and all—entails the attempt to come at the nub of our experience—to catch "the very note and trick", as Henry James would have it, of that experience via "high-raised fantasy", as Milton would have it.

We will have misunderstood Lewis' interests, however, if we think that the scale of those interests is anywhere other than the real, palpable stuff of our human life here on this planet. He does not beckon us away from our experience in his fiction. Rather, he attempts to illumine that experience with the strong light used for many centuries by bards, and left unused for some time now.

We may see this in the scene in which Ransom returns to Earth. He has been asleep as the spaceship approaches, and when he awakes it has landed and Weston and Devine have disembarked and are gone. He hears a drumming noise. "Suddenly his heart gave a great leap. 'Oh God,' he sobbed. 'Oh God! It's *rain.*'" He disembarks, "drinking great draughts of air". Slipping in the mud, he "blessed the smell of it ... stood in pitch-black night under torrential rain. With every pore of his body he drank it in." This is his native terrain, the region we mortals were made for, the very textures of which say "home" to us. "With every desire of his heart he embraced the smell of the field about him—a patch of his native planet where grass grew, where cows moved, where presently he would come to hedges and a gate." Then it is a lane, a road, a village street, a lighted door, voices speaking English, a familiar smell, and Ransom ordering a pint of bitter. This is the very turf of Lewis' fiction.

In every tale Lewis writes, we find ourselves returning and returning, no matter what glories and terrors have regaled us, to lanes and puddles and sandwiches and tea and hearths and pints of beer. Bright fixities and ineffable immensities may arch over our lives, but we live those lives and are at home, for now anyway, in this plain landscape we call Earth. No doubt the lanes and hearthstones of this Earth present us (on this accounting) with smallish adumbrations of the great and utterly satisfying "at-homeness" for which we and all creatures are made. And no doubt the scenes enacted in these lanes and at these hearthsides constitute (on this accounting) some sort of early lessons in the customs of that final home country. But here again, we find ourselves in a region where the language of fiction and that of vision, and indeed of morality, run together. And it is only imagination that will furnish any sort of visibility and integrity to this apparent blur.

In Malacandra, far from being a sort of conquistador, as the busy and humorless Weston fancies himself to be, Ransom finds himself the object of a sort of judgment that may be said to be in the very air. The colors seem to redefine for him the whole notion of color. The contours seem to constitute some sort of "perpendicular theme" in relation to which everything Ransom has ever known seems slightly off plumb. At one point in his adventures, when he is exploring an island, we find this: "He said to himself that he was having a look at the island, but his feeling was rather that the island was having a look at him."[11] And the creatures here: they are neither savage nor ignorant nor churlish. They are different. There seems to be implanted in Ransom's (and our) imagination the seed of an idea that has long since been extinguished in Weston, and indeed in the imagination of all the denizens of Earth with the possible exception of saints and poets and children, that we are neither supreme nor alone in this universe.

[11] Ibid., p. 108.

But again, for the purpose of Lewis' tale, the dramatic center is not to be found in the curiosity attaching to interplanetary travelers encountering strange species. That of course is boundlessly interesting. But here is the language in which we find Ransom's encounter with one of the new creatures described: "It was foolish, frightening, ecstatic and unbearable all in one moment. It was more than curiosity. It was like a courtship—like the meeting of the first man and the first woman in the world." But it was more: it was "the first tingling intercourse of two different, but rational, species".[12]

Certainly at least two things constitute the drama here. First, how shall we reintroduce into human imagination the long-lost notion of blissful otherness, so much a part of the substance of myth? Perhaps we can do it by locating the drama, not in the drawing room or the bedroom, but rather in some region where blissful and wholly other selves may be met. What would an experience like that be *like*? (What was it like for Hamlet to see the ghost?) And second, there is at work here something closer in to ordinary experience, namely, the supposition of a capacity to greet other selves—*any* other selves—with reticence, shyness, courtesy, and honor.

At once we realize that Weston is incapable of this, either in Malacandra or on Earth. Ransom, with no special training in interplanetary decorum, has the ability to react thus. Is this because of innate modesty? Training at home and at school? A capacity for awe? No doubt it contains elements of all three. But the difference between these two capacities is the difference between charity and egoism. We are seeing something of the sort of man each man is, and this is vivified by the whole setting. The drama touches on fine

[12] Ibid., p. 56.

distinctions of behavior and capacity, which turn out to be major, since they thicken and harden into salvation or damnation. After all, Achilles' heel had only a very small bad place on it.

All of Ransom's experiences in Malacandra constitute a sort of litmus paper, we might say, which reveals the nature of the thing we are testing, in this case what it is to be human—what it really is. For example, in so small an aside as Ransom's "not very reasonable astonishment" that the *hross* should have a boat, and that the boat should be not unlike *our* boats: "only later did he set himself the question, 'What else could a boat be like?'" A small aside, but carrying with it enormous philosophical curiosities that reach to Plato and beyond, namely the sense in which our world may be held to supply us with a faithful index as to what Reality is like. Is there not a notion of *boat-hood* to which boats in all possible worlds must approximate? If so, the universe is trustworthy. If not, we must conclude with the existentialist that all is at sixes and sevens, and hence absurd.

Or again, things are well enough as long as Ransom, sitting by the water next to the *hross*, is able to conceive of the creature as an animal, "with everything an animal ought to have—glossy coat, liquid eye, sweet breath and whitest teeth—and added to all these, as though Paradise had never been lost and earliest dreams were true, the charm of speech and reason." [13] But if he tries to think of the *hross* as a sort of human *manqué* because of its rationality, then everything seems grotesque.

One of the things that becomes clear in the course of Ransom's encounters with the three sorts of creatures in Malacandra is his human obsession with questions of power

[13] Ibid., p. 58.

and superiority. One of these three species has got, he thinks, to enjoy the hegemony. It takes some shuffling of his Thulcandrian categories before he gets it clear that the *sorns*, although they are the tallest and clearly the most analogous to our ideas of pure intellect, are not necessarily the master race. "No one learns the *sorns*' speech", a *pfifltrigg* (one of the "artisan" class of creature, rather like what gnomes are in our own world) tells Ransom, "for you can change their knowledge into any words and it is still the same." The *hrossa*, on the other hand, " 'are our great speakers and singers. They have more words and better.... The *hrossa* have furry names like Hnoh and Hnihi and Hyoi and Hlithnahi.' 'The best poetry, then, comes in the roughest speech?' " asks Ransom (and we may recall here Lewis' love of Old English and its poetry). " 'Perhaps,' said the *pfifltrigg*. 'As the best pictures are made in the hardest stone.' "

Lewis is obviously building into the Malacandrian order of things something of what lurks in our own consciousness, and suffuses our myths and our art, about the ways available to us creatures for catching and articulating Reality. There is pure intellect—sheer, celestial logic and fact. We come at it with our rational powers, but full mastery on this front seems reserved for the angels. And there is poetry, whose medium is language, which we work away at, and which a solitary Homer or Dante or Shakespeare seems to approach. And there is craftsmanship, whose medium is gold and stone and pigment, and a very few of us manage to elicit something true about things from this angle. What might it look like if all this that is implicit in our bungling and limited capacities, and that flashes out in an Aristotle, a Dante, or a Vermeer now and again—what might it look like if all this were freely enjoyed and exercised by everyone? Ransom comes upon some such state of affairs in Malacandra, and it is vivified for him in the very forms of the three creatures: the tall, pale, gangling *séroni*, the otterlike *hrossa*, and the busy, burrowing *pfifltriggi*. What is only dimly and intermittently to be descried in our own race is here embodied and enacted in the cleanest colors.

It is through his contact with one of the *pfifltriggi* that Ransom glimpses something of what is meant by our planet being called Thulcandra, the "silent" planet. Later, in conversation with the Oyarsa (the presiding *eldil*, or spirit) of Malacandra, Ransom learns the story of how this silence fell, and it sounds very like our story of the fall of Lucifer because it is that story. Twice in telling the story the Oyarsa uses the phrase "it is a thing we desire to look into". As it happens this is *ipsissima verba* the language of the Authorized Version of 1 Peter 1:12, where we are told that the story of our (human) salvation is a thing the angels "desire to look into". The Oyarsa is not an allegory for an angel, any more than the *hross'* boat was an allegory for our boats: it is simply that we are seeing emerge in another landscape a case in point of what we see in our own. There are certainly *analogues* between one world and another—there have to be, unless the universe is a random clutter.

But to make one world a mere allegory of another would be to dishonor it. Ransom is studying a monolith made by the *pfifltriggi*, and on it he finds a picture of what turns out to be our solar system. On each planet there rides a little winged figure. One holds a trumpet: it is Mercury. Another seems to have udders or breasts: it is Venus. The third has a blank where the figure might be: it is Earth, which has cut itself off from the Dance enjoyed by the other planets and their tutelary intelligences. "'And what an extraordinary coincidence,' thought Ransom, 'that their mythology, like ours, associates some idea of the female with Venus.'" No, not at all extraordinary, if we are following the sense of the drama. If there is Venus at all, then she will look the same in all possible worlds. Lewis carries this imagery through to completion in *Perelandra*.

It is very much as though Ransom is being sent to school in Malacandra. He is the pupil. Ironically, the "scientist" Weston has no curiosity whatever about this world. He is entirely blinded by his prior fixation on the megalomaniacal theories which he has chosen to adopt. Ransom, who has no particular axe to grind, is in a position to learn something. There is a question of teachability at work in the drama, which is of course a subdivision of the larger theme of hubris versus modesty or humility. Another case in point of this is the transfiguring of Ransom's view of the *sorns*. At first they seem threatening and grotesquely awkward to him. But with the clearing of his vision, they seem more "like full-rigged ships before a fair wind. 'Ogres' he had called them when they first met his eyes. . . . 'Titans' or 'Angels' he now thought would have been a better word. . . . He had thought them spectral when they were only august." [14]

It turns out in the judgment before the Oyarsa that Ransom has not been altogether teachable, however, and that he is culpable for certain very small refusals on his own part—refusals that any halfhearted attempt at self-defense would leap at as entirely innocent. But in the serene and implacable light of sheer fact, which seems to be the order of things in the Oyarsa's presence, all sorts of semiconscious missteps and quite well-intentioned detours turn out to be blameworthy. Weston's dronings and posturings dwindle and shrivel to their proper size here. They are imbecilic and, above all, boring. Lewis has chosen the dramatic technique

[14] Ibid., p. 101.

of having Ransom translate Weston's gibberings into the speech of Malacandra, and in this phraseology what seemed important and impressive in Weston's mouth and from his point of view emerges as silly at best and blasphemous at worst.

In a visit with the *sorns*, Ransom learns a bit about hierarchy, and it is an idea wholly unlike our (Thulcandrian) ideas of power struggle. He finds that the *sorns*, astonished at his account of human wars and slavery, conclude either that humans have no Oyarsa ruling them, or more probably that all this trouble is because each one wants to be a little oyarsa himself. Over against this is the Malacandrian scheme of things, in which each order is ruled by the next higher order: beasts by *hnau* (intelligent beings), *hnau* by *eldila*, and *eldila* by Maleldil, the lord of it all. Creatures cannot rule themselves: it is like trying to lift oneself by one's own hair.

And Ransom finds everyone on Malacandra slightly perplexed by the Thulcandrian obsession with "lifting and carrying things". Indeed, they have a law, it seems, never to speak much of sizes or numbers. In this light, somehow the entire scientific and mercantile enterprise seems to dwindle. Further, Ransom finds that these creatures are bemused by there being only one sort of intelligent life on Thulcandra: "they thought this must have far-reaching effects in the narrowing of sympathy and even of thought." [15] The ancient poets may have known what they were doing after all in peopling their tales with fauns and gods and dryads and titans as well as men.

At one point Ransom, who has several times noticed regions of ancient forest in Malacandra which are now

[15] Ibid., p. 103.

unpeopled, thinks about these and about "what it might mean to grow up seeing always so few miles away a land of colour that could never be reached and had once been inhabited".[16] The only analogy, perhaps, from our Thulcandrian experience for an experience like this would be that of reading the myths, which point us to once-inhabited but now inaccessible landscapes, and in so doing, plant in us a certain *tentativeness* of attitude about our own familiar scenes. There is more, they seem to murmur. Your story is *part* of the story. Live in the awareness of that. It is salutary.

And from the *hrossa* Ransom learns something about pleasure—how it is full-grown only when it is remembered, and how this remembering is itself the fruition of the pleasure. The *hrossa*, for instance, do not keep on copulating throughout their lives: that is a pleasure appropriate specifically to the time of child-bearing; there is no question of endless repetition. There is something incomprehensible, from the *hrossa*'s point of view, about the mere repeating of pleasures such as hearing a lovely line of poetry over and over. "For the most splendid line becomes fully splendid only by means of all the lines after it; if you went back to it you would find it less splendid than you thought. You would kill it."[17]

We find this theme appearing again and again in Lewis' fiction, under many modalities; and it always implies that at least part of the key to the nature of evil is that it is a refusal of fact—the fact that obliges us to stay with the story as it moves toward its denouement, and that will not allow dawdling and detour. The amassing of money, for example, by miserliness or thievery, would represent one variation

[16] Ibid.
[17] Ibid., p. 73.

on this theme, for the only thing money can do is to guarantee (we think) some sort of repetition of pleasure, and the warding off of contingency. By the same token, sexual promiscuity would represent the mere amassing of pleasurable experiences, with no regard for how the pleasure fits into the total pattern of human life; or again, gluttony or drunkenness would be variations on this theme of the mere repetition of pleasure to the point of surfeit.

Perhaps one way of saying what Lewis' achievement is in *Out of the Silent Planet* would be to say that he has pressed the genre "space fiction" into the service of ancient mythic and poetic themes—so much so that the designation "space fiction" no longer really applies very well, since at least part of what has occurred in the drama has been the waking up, from its merely scientific torpor, of our notion of what space is. The shift from space to Deep Heaven, though, is itself only in the service of the higher theme, which is, surely, that there is a Story afoot in all worlds, and that to "escape" from the silence of our own world into the clarity and luminescence of another may be to find ourselves suddenly face to face with our own story, only in a clearer light and with starker colors.

CHAPTER FOUR

Perelandra:
The Paradoxes of Joy

One of the obvious properties of fairy tale or myth, as we have pointed out, is the way everything is visible, literal, and explicit. The elements that might be merely psychological or metaphorical or implicit in realistic narratives appear quite unabashedly as real people or places or situations in a fairy tale or a myth. In a fairy tale you find yourself, not in a psychological "dark forest" that is really only a patch of perplexity or discouragement: you get into a real Black Forest with great gnarled beeches and willows all gaunt and bearded, reaching their knotted limbs down at you. In a myth you do not find yourself with mere "herculean" labors to do: you find a real Hercules having to clean out the Augean Stables or behead the Hydra. You don't have an emotional or intellectual Achilles' heel in a myth: your heel really is vulnerable, right at the small place on it that did not get immersed when your mother dipped you into the Styx.

We find this property in Lewis' fiction. It is as though he ignores the frontier between "realism" and fantasy. The difficult thing at this point for criticism is that our own era tends to identify this sort of realism with "serious" fiction, and to identify fantasy with "unimportant" fiction. Some twentieth-century writers have toyed along this frontier, however: Henry James dances on the border with *The Turn of the Screw*, as though to taunt us all with "*Are* there ghosts here or not?" and Kafka with his cockroach does likewise.

The irony for our own era is that most of the "serious" works of human imagination lie on the far side of that border in the realm of fantasy. Zeus and Satan and Grendel and ghosts and dragons romp all through the stories over there, and all those stories seem to be "important". No one can spell out exactly the reasons for our deciding that we must all stay on the hither side of the border now.

Lewis was aware of discussions like this. Who could be a teacher of English in a modern university and not be aware of it? His interest in his fiction, next to the central interest of simply telling a good story, was to see how things might look, not so much if you ignore the border, as if you deny altogether that it exists. In other words, what sort of a story will you get if you release the dragons and the gods from their exile and admit them once again into the hither realm of the "real" and the "serious"? What will your story look like if you have a plain modern man struggling not just against dehumanizing *ideas* but against the real thing of which those ideas are the merest shadow? What if you reverse the angle of vision, as it were, or the eyepiece, so that imagination looks through the other end of the glass now—the end through which Homer and Isaiah and others peered? What looks real then? What looks serious then?

We may say that something like this is at work in Lewis' narrative technique. His story simply moves out from the rather small corral in which fiction now ordinarily pens itself, into regions where we encounter not just Wellsian monsters or space technology, but the living realities amongst which human imagination ranged before it was penned in.

Perelandra, like *Out of the Silent Planet* before it, begins with the reasonable figure of Ransom. His experience of blundering into distances and immensities that have formed no part of his quiet scholar's life hitherto is the vehicle within which we enter the narrative. His incredulity and even irritation upon finding himself whisked into these fantastic regions establishes a bridge of credibility between our vantage point and these narratives. The drama anticipates us, as it were, by exclaiming before we have the chance, "Great Scott! This can't be serious!" At least part of Lewis' achievement is that his fiction stretches our capacity to imagine certain forgotten dimensions or aspects of experience. By the technique of dragooning a sensible modern man like Ransom into these fantastic regions, Lewis enables us to see experience once again in a light similar to the light in which it was seen by all human imagination until the modern era.

Perelandra carries the action further than does *Out of the Silent Planet*. It is not simply a matter of going farther into space (Venus is farther out than Mars). We are farther into Deep Heaven, dramatically, we might say. What was encountered in only an introductory sort of way in *Out of the Silent Planet* is here pressed into the service of higher drama. It may be analogous to the difference between the kind of drama you get in *Romeo and Juliet* and what you get in *Measure for Measure*. In the former there is certainly plenty of excitement and peril and emotion; but it all seems a bit thin when you compare it with the more mature achievement in *Measure for Measure* where the excitement and peril and emotion attach, not to chance and Fate and near-misses (as they do in *Romeo and Juliet*), but rather to the tension that arises in the human spirit when its cavalier moral claims run afoul of moral conundrums that do not seem to admit of any very clear answer. In other words, the more immature the art, the more it may depend on external machinery like Fate and coincidence and hugger-mugger liaisons; the more mature the art, the more it must locate the drama in the fatal and unmanageable ambiguities we find in our own souls.

This line of thought would seem to have run us straight into the cul-de-sac of saying, "Well, there you have it: Lewis' narratives depend on all kinds of wild interplanetary machinery for their effects. On that accounting it is immature art." The point here, though, is that all this interplanetary machinery, including the ravishing vistas and awesome creatures, is not there to intensify the pressure or raise the level of excitement. It is, rather, the fabric, or locale, necessary to the drama itself. It is not just a question of outwitting Martians or conquering Venus: it is that the narratives force us to see with startlingly fresh intensity the very outlines and colors of a drama that is all too recognizable to us earthly mortals. Like Hercules' struggle with the Hydra, the very farfetchedness supplies the stark perspective in which we suddenly recognize the plain truth about our own experience.

But the claim being made here is not that Lewis' space trilogy is to be juxtaposed with Shakespeare's mature art, but that just as you can see in the progression from one play to another a ripening of the storyteller's art, so it would seem to be in the progression from the first to the second of these two novels. The *nature* of the drama has intensified while the milieu in both cases remains similar (Verona and Venice in the two Shakespeare plays; Mars and Venus in the two Lewis stories).

For one thing, *Perelandra* is not nearly so "episodic" as *Out of the Silent Planet*. In the earlier narrative we move from wonder to wonder: first away from Earth, then across the face of Malacandra, meeting one by one the denizens of that place, each of whom exhibits some special excellence. And all the while there is the external pressure of wondering what Weston may be up to.

In *Perelandra* the drama builds more "organically". We are back once again in a landscape whose contours, textures, and colors elicit from Ransom not only awe and delight at new sights but also an intensifying of desire for *more than this*. The nature of beauty in Perelandra seems to be not only to awaken desire and reward it with pleasure, but then to nudge one ever on—not clamoring for more and more of this (that would be cupidity) but rather inquiring and inquiring what it all may mean (as does sanctity). The taste of this fruit: there is something about it that seems to say, "There. That is pure delight. Be filled. But do not suppose that you will double your pleasure by eating two. Glut and surfeit lie that way, and those are servants of stupefaction which itself is the servant of death and hell." (This, of course, is to carry the language too suddenly into the vocabulary of theology and ethics. It is difficult to avoid doing this, but for the moment at least it must be avoided if we are to stay with the narrative Lewis has given us. If our pleasure lies in darting about, seizing upon this and that and saying, "Aha! I've found the moral equivalent for that one!" then we might as well have a cryptogram or a riddle. Those are indeed forms of diversion and therefore of pleasure: but they are not exactly of the same order as the pleasure afforded by fiction.)

We may watch the organic unfolding of the drama in this narrative by watching Ransom's progress not so much from incident to incident as from lesser capacity to greater, toward fuller, deeper, clearer awareness of what is happening. We move from the curious to the frightening to the beautiful to the ravaging and terrifying and finally to the utterly serene and ecstatic.

The narrative begins, not with Ransom at all, but with Lewis the narrator. Certainly at least part of what is achieved here (compare Joseph Conrad with his narrator Marlow) is twofold: first, a certain distance and vantage point from which we may begin to get our bearings; and second, a certain identification point for us. The Ransom whom we are going to encounter presently is already an "initiate" so to speak; but this Lewis is only a bystander like us. The difficulties he encounters on the three-mile walk from the railway station at Worchester to Ransom's cottage take the form of doubt, fear, self-pity, and plain irritation. He seems to be struggling against a headwind. As it turns out, this is all a "barrage". What Lewis has experienced as just a sequence of rather jumbled feelings and thoughts which, taken all together seem to add up to general discouragement and vexation, turns out upon Ransom's explanation to be "they"—the *eldila*—those beings analogous to angels in other stories. This time it is the bad *eldila*, and the drama thickens.

It has been a full-dress temptation scene, and we are embarked upon the main concern of the drama. We may say that this concern is temptation, since the whole drama turns upon the question as to how we might imagine a situation analogous to our own world's Fall, the difference being that this time the Fall is averted. But of course there is a sense in which the word "temptation" will not quite compass the business since temptation itself immediately implies bigger questions, namely, what is the nature of a world in which temptation occurs, and what does it imply about things that temptation should be permitted at all, and what is the nature of the Good that there should be this attractive and counterfeit alternative to it, and how does Evil go about making its bid, and so forth. So that to say that the main concern in *Perelandra* is temptation is to say that the action occurs in a certain kind of world and that the drama entails tensions implicit in the very fabric of that world. If there is all this beauty and harmony and serenity, why should anyone want anything else, or be in the least susceptible to the suggestion of alternatives?

The great struggle is over whether Weston will be able to haul this world, in the person of Tinidril, over to disobedience and ruin, or whether Ransom will be able to ward off the catastrophe. It is clearly going to come to somebody's *opting* for the Good, pure and simple, over against Weston's whole program, which is overridingly plausible and vastly desirable when compared with the rather limiting and unprogressive nature of the scheme to which Tinidril is obedient.

This is one of the ironies often appearing in Lewis' fiction, that perfection itself (life in Perelandra in this case) can be made to seem confining and demeaning and boring by the sullen alchemy of evil. Dissatisfaction, sailing under false colors of liberation and ambition and progress, is the flagship in Weston's flotilla, as it were. And it eventually becomes clear that this dissatisfaction with what is given stands at the polar opposite to the obedience and contentment exhibited in people like the Beavers and the *hrossa* and, later, the Dimbles. It is a wanting to know the "what would have been" that Aslan always refuses to grant, and the desire to peer into someone else's story. In the world of Malacandra and Perelandra (and Narnia), it appears that acceptance of the given, and submission to it, is the key to contentment. Paradoxically, of course, contrary to the accusations of all Nietzschean and Promethean romantics like Uncle Andrew and Jadis and Weston that this is all an opiate, this submission is synonymous with freedom and maturity. It is analogous to one's submission to the steps of a minuet or to swimming instructions: here is how it is done, and if you want to know the lovely freedom of dancing and swimming, you must do it this way. The same bright alchemy that transforms rules and obedience into freedom and joy here can also be seen at work in all gymnasts and ballet dancers and poets and athletes. They have all learned how it is done. If it is objected here that this is the very recipe itself for bondage and that on this accounting all tyrants may brutalize the creatures under their rule, it may be pointed out that it is the nature of evil, alas, to ape the good. The tyranny of the Witch is the parody of Aslan's absolute rule. The oppression and sadism at Belbury, or in the person of Trom of Glome, are grotesque travesties of what we find in Aslan, or at St. Anne's, or under Queen Orual's rule, where we find authority coupled with its necessary corollaries, wisdom and goodness and charity.

But we do not stumble upon all this at once in the narrative in *Perelandra*. As in any good drama there is a rising intensity, with harbingers sounding warnings ahead of time. The relatively small temptation that Lewis runs into in the first scene is not so much a matter of his being invited to pursue a fraudulent good the way Edmund or Eustace were tempted to do, as of his running into plain resistance. Like all temptation, it appears to be merely an interior matter— just a state of nerves or a matter of making sensible choices or of following reasonable inclinations. It does not reveal itself at all as outside opposition. The thing which this sort of temptation has in common with the more deadly types is that both represent a deflecting from the first good—a veering from true north, say, or a getting off plumb. In Lewis' case here it is "merely" a matter of perhaps going back on a rather small commitment—his agreement to pop down to Ransom's cottage and give him a hand. Nothing much is at stake. To go back would not matter in the least. But in the light of the rest of the drama in this narrative, this very small business is thrown into very high relief. Lewis is being tempted to choose something other than the good of duty (always a rather pedestrian good—not at all your exciting forms of good), and the point is that he has no way of knowing at this juncture just how much is at stake. Just a small deflection is presented to him, and all of plausibility is on its side.

The thing which saves him here is sheer decency—as he puts it, "some rag of sanity and some reluctance to let Ransom down". This is a far cry from the waving banner of some more obviously heroic charge into the ranks of temptation, but this is what it comes down to here: merely the old, plodding schoolboy convention of keeping your commitments and one thing and another.

We find this again and again in the narrative—this way in which the business of resisting temptation must be got through as often as not without any dramatic help. When Lewis mentions his difficulties to Ransom presently, Ransom explains that, since it was the bad *eldila* who were opposing Lewis, "the best plan is to take no notice and keep straight on. Don't try to answer them. They like drawing you into an interminable argument." [1] The danger to be avoided, as seen here and elsewhere in Lewis' narratives (in *The Silver Chair*, for

[1] C. S. Lewis, *Perelandra* (New York: Macmillan Publishing Company, 1965), p. 21.

example), is wasting time discussing something that you know, or at least have known, to be true, as though there were some question about it. If it is clear today that you are supposed to leave Ur of the Chaldees, for example, then no concatenation of bad weather, truculent camels, surly drivers, and harrying marauders ought to make you raise the question again. By the same token, if it is laid down that fornication is interdicted, then all symposia and colloquia and round tables and seminars which have for their agenda the reopening of the question under the vocabulary of "meaningful relationships" and "reassessing of traditional morality" are a waste of time and pernicious. At least this would be the case given the serenely fixed moral structure of the world Lewis evokes in his fiction—and, he might add, in all possible worlds: if something is true, then that's that. You shouldn't keep fiddling with the latch to see if there might not be some method other than the key to get it open. No doubt there is, but only picklocks do that sort of thing.

When Lewis asks Ransom if he feels happy about his imminent voyage to Perelandra in the coffinlike vehicle, Ransom draws upon a similar line of thought.

> *If you mean, Does my reason accept the view that [the eldil] will (accidents apart) deliver me safe on the surface of Perelandra?—the answer is Yes.... If you mean, Do my nerves and my imagination respond to this view?—I'm afraid the answer is No. One can believe in anesthetics and yet feel in a panic when they actually put the mask over your face. I think I feel as a man who believes in the future life feels when he is taken out to face a firing party. Perhaps it's good practice.*[2]

[2] Ibid., p. 27.

Here it is again—this brisk, no-nonsense approach to ordeals and testings. We have a variation on this when it comes down to Lewis packing Ransom in the "coffin" for the voyage. Because there are the instructions, and because he has agreed to help, this is what must be done: but that sparse fare is absolutely all that seems available for his wayward imagination to feed on. "I had no thoughts of the planet Venus now and no real belief that I should see him again. If I had dared I would have gone back on the entire scheme".[3] Except that there is one other factor: the *eldil* who has brought the instructions seems to be "there", if an *eldil* can be said to be in any location, "and the fear of it was upon me." Fear—not a very virtuous or heroic sentiment—is there to assist.

In this first scene Lewis has his first experience of an *eldil*. He has, of course, learned of these beings from Ransom's accounts of his trip to Malacandra. Lewis' encounter here strikes a note which sets the key for the narrative. That is, his experience of the *eldil* throws the sum total of his human, sensuous experience, not into a cocked hat, but rather into some sort of *perspective*. It becomes clear that there are dimensions, or modes, of reality which are mediated to us by sensuous experience (taste, smell, feel, sound, color) but which are by no means limited to these sensuous qualities. For instance, in this scene, when Lewis stumbles into Ransom's cottage and is groping about trying to get a match struck, he hears Ransom's name pronounced: ". . . but I should not like to say I heard a voice pronounce it. The sound was quite astonishingly unlike a voice. It was perfectly articulate: it was even, I suppose, rather beautiful. But it was, if you understand me, inorganic."[4] He goes on

[3] Ibid., p. 29.
[4] Ibid., p. 17.

to point out at some length that "voice" for us mortals implies the whole machinery of blood and lungs and "the warm, moist cavity of the mouth", but that this does not exhaust the notion of voice. But this sound which he heard, while it was *more* articulate than what we mortals can produce when we voice words, was not mechanical: "this was more as if rock or crystal or light had spoken of itself."

Then he sees "a very faint rod or pillar of light". So far so good. We are at liberty to conjure up an image of a sort of thin, straight specter. But then there is trouble—its color, for one thing. Since Lewis saw it, he must have seen it as either white or colored, he says. But his great difficulty is that no *color*—blue, gold, violet, red—will suffice. It was more, not less, than our notions of color will answer to. And the angle: it seemed to define an absolute perpendicular in relation to which every angle in the cottage and indeed on Earth was slightly out of kilter.

All this is explained by the narrator Lewis in the story, not Lewis the author sitting in his rooms at Magdalen speculating about things. It is not a sort of metaphysical or astrological footnote included to ginger up the story or divert our fancies with a speculative detour. It is what the story is *about*. The whole drama involves this encounter with things that are *truer* than our ordinary apprehension of things.

Two observations may be made here. First, the slight scepticism and incredulity of this narrator keeps the story itself from flying altogether out of our grasp into the realm of wild fancy, where we have nothing but marvel piled upon marvel in a sheer tumult of adventure. The narrator's own difficulties provide a sort of narrative anchor. And second, the fresh apprehension of things which this encounter with "truer" things affords shows the particular way in which myth does its work. All forms of narrative—epic, ballad, novel, short story—have their own genius here, but each one has for its end the rendering of sober justice to the truth of our experience.

But what sober justice can possibly be rendered by a description of these encounters with *eldila*? Surely they are merely fantastic creations in a fantastic narrative?

We may answer yes to this latter question with two reservations. First, perhaps the word "merely" could be struck: it is always a dangerous business to apply the word "mere" to any element you see in an artist's work. Did Michelangelo run out of ideas and *merely* have his David's hand hanging down rather limply that way? Did Vermeer *merely* happen to have the light coming through that window that way? And second, perhaps we may make sure we understand the word "fantastic" to mean, not "nonsensical" or "trivial", but rather, "highly imagined". What sober justice to our experience is gained by having this sort of creature appear in a piece of adult fiction?

We may follow Lewis' own reactions to seeing the *eldil* by way of coming at an answer. He had at first felt "abject panic" when he heard its words. This panic had organized itself, upon his actually seeing the *eldil*, into a state of being "profoundly disturbed". Then he realizes that his fear was of a special kind:

> *I felt sure that the creature was what we call "good," but I wasn't sure whether I liked "goodness" so much as I had supposed. . . . How if food itself turns out to be the very thing you can't eat, and home the very place you can't live, and your very comforter the person who makes you uncomfortable? Then, indeed, there is no rescue possible: the last card has been played. . . . Here at last was a bit of that world from beyond the world, which I had always supposed*

> *that I loved and desired, breaking through and appearing to*
> *my senses: and I didn't like it, I wanted it to go away. I*
> *wanted every possible distance, gulf, curtain, blanket, and*
> *barrier to be placed between it and me.*[5]

And suddenly, without leaving the narrative for the smallest detour, we find language that comes straight from the borders of moral theology and mystical vision. Aha, we say: there's the real human dilemma. It's glory that we want eventually, and glory is the very thing we can't tolerate. The *eldil*, so utterly pure, is, alas, a herald from the realm of intolerable purity—the realm of sheer Fact. I, being mortal and human, spend my entire time dodging and evading and skirting and fleeing and papering over sheer Fact, so that when I am hailed with it, I find myself paralyzed.

But the point here is not to extract homilies from the narrative. Of course that is the human dilemma. What we want to observe here is that the arrival of this *eldil* on stage does herald the raising of the scrim, so to speak, so that what has hitherto been only dimly perceived behind the small action at Ransom's cottage presently will loom upon us and blot out everything else. You get hints and guesses in the small stage-front action of the drama of which that action is a part. Or put it this way: the scrim does not go up on a *different* drama; rather, by going up it opens out and deepens and illuminates things so that we see them in true perspective. You would have something like this in *King Lear*, for example, where by hauling us out onto the heath and into the tempest, Shakespeare takes us, not *away* from what is going on anyway, but *into* what is going on. The tempest and the heath are the true landscape of that drama.

[5] Ibid., p. 19.

In Ransom's voyage to Perelandra, the action moves into its true locale. We have already been introduced to this phenomenon of a wholly new locale in *Out of the Silent Planet*, and before Ransom departs on this voyage we are reminded of what that experience meant to him:

> *Oh, Lewis . . . I'd give anything I possess . . . just to look down one of those gorges again and see the blue, blue water winding in and out among the woods. . . . It's on hot summer days—looking up at the deep blue and . . . thinking that* in *there, millions of miles deep where I can never, never get back to it, there's a place I know.*[6]

This ravaging desire for that realm that Ransom experiences stands over against the fear that Lewis has just experienced in the presence of a mere herald from that realm. The context in which we see all that happens in Perelandra is Ransom's account to the "earthbound" Lewis of those glories and splendors that have so ravished him and that Lewis so fears. At least part of the drama, then, has entailed Ransom's progress from fear to desire in the presence of the bright realities, and Lewis' posture as a beginner here keeps this before us.

It is possible to see four elements, or stages, in the drama unfolded in Ransom's own account of his experiences in Perelandra. We may designate them this way: the setting; the threat; the struggle; and the denouement. (Almost any drama follows some such pattern as this.)

The setting is something like the mythic landscapes of perfection—the Garden of the Hesperides, or Arcadia, say. Perhaps the key to Ransom's whole desperate effort to

[6] Ibid., p. 22.

describe what he has seen is suggested in an outburst which Lewis recalls from another occasion when a sceptical friend of theirs is pressing Lewis on the absurdity of Lewis' belief in the resurrection of the body. "So you think you're going to have guts and a palate for ever in a world where there'll be no eating, and genital organs in a world without copulation? Man, ye'll have a grand time of it!" [7] Whereupon Ransom intervenes with, "Oh, don't you see, you ass, that there's a difference between a trans-sensuous life and a non-sensuous life?"

The point is that the solid and bright Reality that is guessed at in such hints as food and sex here is not limited to those modalities. Far from it. *They* are the hints: *it* is the real thing. Again, the narrator Lewis recalls a time when he had commented to Ransom, "Of course, I realize it's all rather too vague for you to put into words", and Ransom replies sharply, "On the contrary, it is words that are vague.... It's too *definite* for language." [8]

This is what Ransom encounters in Perelandra. The "prodigious white light"; the rich colors; the pure, flat gold of the sky; the thunder like laughter; the sweet smells—Ransom flounders among such phrases as "prodigality of sweetness" and "unendurable light" in his effort to catch it in words. Every smell and taste and texture is prodigious and unendurable, it seems. We find that Ransom must learn to walk, since the "land" there turns out to be, with one exception, a sort of archipelago of islands floating in the warm and swelling sea, so, like a landlubber staggering across the deck of a clipper ship, he must get his sea legs. We find that he encounters a new kind of hunger and thirst, roused

[7] Ibid., p. 32.
[8] Ibid., p. 33.

in him by the unutterably sweet smells in the forest: it seems to be hunger and thirst that is like "a longing that seemed to flow over from the body into the soul and which was heaven to feel."[9] He tastes some fruit and finds "a new *genus* of pleasures ... out of all reckoning, beyond all covenant. For one draught of this on earth wars would be fought.... It could not be classified."[10]

But he also finds, in this connection, that something seems to warn him off merely repeating the pleasure of eating this fruit. Apparently (he senses) a repetition would be vulgarity. Later, when he discovers some trees which bear globes which, merely touched, burst upon him with a shower of scented bliss, and realizes that he could plunge about in an orgy of pleasure here, he reflects: perhaps the stricture he senses which forbids this orgiastic repetition hints at

> *a principle of far wider application and deeper moment. This itch to have things over again, as if life were a film that could be unrolled twice or even made to work backwards ... was it possibly the root of all evil? No: of course the love of money was called that. But money itself—perhaps one valued it chiefly as a defense against chance, a security of being able to have things over again, a means of arresting the unrolling of the film.*[11]

And there you have once more the theme, encountered a dozen times in Narnia and Malacandra, that you have to stay with the story as it is told by the Author. To tinker with it, or to try to find out if there are alternative ways of getting through the plot, is like finding Hamlet insisting

[9] Ibid., p. 41.
[10] Ibid., p. 42.
[11] Ibid., p. 48.

that Shakespeare does not know what he is doing, with a twofold difference: we, unlike Hamlet, *can* quarrel with the author; and that author, unlike Shakespeare who was only a very great artist, is a Perfect Artist.

We find this theme very much at work in the matter of the Fixed Land on Perelandra: it is forbidden for Tor and Tinidril, the only two human inhabitants of Perelandra, to *remain* on this nonundulating island. Or rather, it is forbidden that they remain there *yet*. Not until they have come into their inheritance as King and Queen of Perelandra and have taken up their sovereignty may they settle on the Fixed Land. Until then, the unpredictability and fluidity of the floating islands, rising and falling on the swells of the sea, will furnish them with good schooling in the thing which will forever obtain, namely their dependence on the Will of Maleldil, arriving and arriving like the waves of the sea. After they have learned that they are entirely secure in the very uncertainty of the floating islands, which are supported in the warm sea the way all things are supported in the Will of Maleldil, then they may graduate to the Fixed Land where they take up new kinds of responsibility. But they must learn first that their only real safety lies, not in an apparent fixity and motionlessness and predictability, but rather in the Will of Maleldil. To insist on an obvious fixity now is like amassing the experiences offered by the globes on the trees or the lovely fruit, or (in Thulcandra) like amassing money: all are ways of shoring things up against contingency and unpredictability.

The net effect of all this on Ransom is to give him the sensation "not of following an adventure but of enacting a myth. To be the figure that he was in this unearthly pattern appeared sufficient." [12] Here he is in this realm of perfect

---

[12] Ibid., p. 47.

harmony, and all would appear to be well: the warm climate is perfect, the fruit of the land seems inexhaustible and more than satisfying to a man's hunger, and he has a small golden-scaled dragon for a sort of mascot. All is well.

Except that presently a human figure appears, racing over the water on the back of a dolphinlike fish. And instantly all else pales. He tries to wave the figure down, but it disappears. "The solitude which up till now had been scarcely painful, had become a horror.... The drugging and entrancing beauty had vanished from his surroundings; take that one human form away and all the rest of this world was now pure nightmare...." [13] He, like Adam, is made for fellowship with his own kind. No mere environment, no matter how edenic, will suffice.

The conversations between Ransom and the Green Lady, or Tinidril (for that is who this figure turns out to be), make explicit the theme that has already appeared in the form of Perelandra itself with its clarity and beauty—the theme, namely, of Reality appearing in forms so different from the forms we are accustomed to on our planet that the juxtaposition of the familiar and the new forms wakes us up, perhaps for the first time, to the dazzling and blissful nature of that Reality. It is not so much that Perelandra is an inexpressibly beautiful world to be pined for (although that is certainly the case), as that both our world, Thulcandra, *and* Perelandra speak of the same Reality which is the fountainhead of all beauty and bliss. One of the themes in the trilogy is that Thulcandra is the Silent Planet, bound, as it were, under some sort of curse because of its disobedience and waiting like the Sleeping Beauty for its awakening.

[13] Ibid., p. 52.

Ransom and the Green Lady speak of time, for example, and it becomes quite clear that Ransom's merely quantitative ideas on this topic do not at all exhaust the matter. The Green Lady's idea is much closer to a qualitative idea— what we might think of when we in our world think of eternity: she, for example, is "older", not by virtue of a unit of a certain measurable length called a day or a night having passed, but rather by virtue of her having *learned* something. She learns from Ransom that time might be a bit like the waves which look one way as they approach, one way when you are in them, and a third way when they have gone past. This observation has the effect, of course, of suggesting to Ransom (and us) that perhaps time (day and night, say) and space (the waves moving over the surface) are both merely modes under which we creatures experience the movement of the Story.

The lady learns self-consciousness from Ransom, and this is a mixed blessing—or at least a dangerous one. Almost all of Ransom's analytical questions and comments seem to her to be a matter of "stepping out of life into the Alongside",[14] as though one were not quite a real character *in* the story but only a spectator. On this view, the analytic or critical faculty in us mortals may grow into the thing we call freedom by enabling us to choose to love the pattern, or it may mushroom into the tumescent and fevered thing which calls itself independence.

Ransom's surprise at discovering a creature in "human" form on this planet, when he had encountered *hrossa*, *sorns*, and *pfifltriggi* in Malacandra, makes very little sense to the Lady: after all, she points out, Malacandra was an *older* planet than Thulcandra, and since Maleldil took on human form

---

[14] Ibid., p. 60.

in Thulcandra, "how should Reason in any world take on another form?"[15] Time, as it were, has turned a corner "and everything this side of it is new."

Ransom expresses surprise that such a huge event as that should have occurred on one little world like his, and once more the Lady expresses surprise over his obsession with size: that is a mere matter of measurement, or quantity. What has that got to do with anything? The farther we get in the narrative, the more our whole terrestrial way of looking at everything recedes, enabling us to get some perspective on it. Obviously there are ways of accounting for things that pay not the slightest attention to how big or how expensive things are. There is an order of things in which the things that are not are chosen to bring to naught the things that are, and in which the rich get sent empty away and strength is ordained from the mouths of babes and sucklings and imperial armies are scattered and a colt, the foal of an ass, is a king's charger. None of this would surprise the Green Lady in Perelandra, but it is hard for Ransom, coming from a world where they want to know how much and how far and how big and how many and how expensive—for him to relearn this ordering of things.

As yet, Ransom has no way of coping with the quality that he perceives in the Green Lady: his earthly mind casts about among goddesses (she is "beautiful, naked, shameless, young") and madonnas ("the face so calm that it escaped insipidity by the very concentration of its mildness") and children, for something to anchor his imagination with respect to her. She has no "identity", if by that we mean what we on Earth usually mean, namely a family and biography and a list of achievements. Ransom finds that there is

[15] Ibid., p. 62.

a King, the only other human being on Perelandra. Who is he? He is the King: "How can one answer such a question?"[16] Well, what about your mother? "What do you mean? I *am* the Mother." And there is no mistaking the source of the echo in her words that follow: "Only my spirit praises Maleldil who comes down from Deep Heaven into this lowness and will make me to be blessed by all the times that are rolling towards us. It is He who is strong and makes me strong and fills empty worlds with good creatures."[17] There is a song in our own story like that, called Magnificat. And when, presently, this great Lady and Mother and Queen sends greetings via Ransom to the Lady and Mother on Thulcandra, we find this: "And now for the first time there was a note of deliberate courtesy, even of ceremony, in her speech. Ransom understood. She knew now at last that she was not addressing an equal. She was a queen sending a message to a queen through a commoner, and her manner to him was hence forward more gracious."[18] How has she learned this protocol? She hasn't. Rather, protocol here in our world is the learned thing which echoes the courtesies that run up and down the hierarchy of all worlds. In Perelandra we see the hierarchy peacefully and joyously at work. The beasts follow the Lady ("Do the beasts not follow in your world?"[19] Alas—they did at the outset, but we broke our contract and now there is enmity). And, she explains to Ransom, upon his question as to whether there are not *eldila* in Perelandra, that, "since our Beloved became a Man", the sovereignty has passed to human hands, and the *eldila* have grown less as we increased. It is their special

[16] Ibid., p. 66.
[17] Ibid.
[18] Ibid., p. 67.
[19] Ibid., p. 77.

joy to cherish and help us and bring us to our maturity and inheritance, "till they could fall at our feet. It is a joy we shall not have. However I teach the beasts they will never be better than I. But it is a joy beyond all. Not that it is better joy than ours. Every joy is beyond all others. The fruit we are eating is always the best fruit of all." [20] Here Ransom must mention to her that there was an *eldil* in our world who did not like this ordering of things, and who is stuck forever clinging to the "old good", as it were, of his original supremacy over mankind, thus turning that good into rottenness.

Ransom has perceived that "her purity and peace were not, as they had seemed, things settled and inevitable like the purity and peace of an animal—that they were alive and therefore breakable ... able to be lost." [21] And in a moment an alarming possibility looms: the Lady muses over Ransom's question to her about her "disappointment" at discovering that it was he, a stranger, and not the King, her spouse, waving to her when they first met. She reflects on this business of the expected good and the given good, and sees that one always sets aside, so to speak, the good *not* given at the split second when the given good is given. But "you could send your soul after the good you had expected, instead of turning it to the good you had got. You could refuse the real good; you could make the real fruit taste insipid by thinking of the other." [22] She sees the glory of choice—of willing to receive the given good and set aside the one not given, thus staying in step with actuality. But again, "One can conceive a heart which did not: which clung to the good it had first thought of and turned the

[20] Ibid., p. 83.
[21] Ibid., p. 68.
[22] Ibid., p. 69.

good which was given it into no good." [23] And, having discovered this, she realizes that it is hers to *walk with* Maleldil, not simply be carried in his Will. "The going itself is the path." [24]

For the hundredth time in Lewis' fiction we are encountering the theme. It is, of course, the old theme of human freedom, choice, obedience, goodness, the will of God, and of how these all harmonize in any sort of pattern. The Lady is moving along a track that was laid out for us on Thulcandra to follow, but which we left before we had hardly started.

This, then, is the setting: innocence, splendor, and unsullied peace.

But then the threat. Weston, the fiercely megalomaniacal scientific utopian who was the antagonist in *Out of the Silent Planet*, appears once more, landing in his spaceship. He will carry his program from star to star, to the end of the universe. He will override "the vast astronomical distances which are God's quarantine regulations", pursuing "the sweet poison of the false infinite".[25] Ransom now realizes for the first time why he has been sent to Perelandra: he must interpose himself between this innocent, vulnerable world and Weston's attempt at conquest.

The only word which will suffice to describe the ambience that Weston drags with him is filth. His revolver, his assumption that the Green Lady is a "native" (she is, but not in the way Weston uses the word), and his conclusion that the spectacle of the naked Lady with the naked Ransom can mean only fornication—it is all filthy, and infinitely wearisome. Almost immediately he gives Ransom the account

[23] Ibid.
[24] Ibid., p. 70.
[25] Ibid., p. 81.

of his intellectual and spiritual odyssey—no doubt a bracing testimony in his eyes, but somehow it comes through as being fathomlessly tedious. From physics to biology to the utility of the human race to the utility of all of Nature to the conclusion that "All is one.... The majestic spectacle of this blind, inarticulate purposiveness thrusting its way upward and ever upward ... the forward movement of Life—the growing spirituality ... to spread spirituality, not to spread the human race, is henceforth my mission." [26] Indeed, he condescendingly agrees with all of Ransom's ideas, give or take "a few outworn theological technicalities". We cannot avoid hearing the echo here of Uncle Andrew and the ape Shift, and all Bergsonians and scientific materialist visionaries, and all diabolically romantic utopians. On and on, a great regurgitation of noisome, polysyllabic idealism until we reach the inevitable: "In so far as I am the conductor of the central forward pressure of the universe, I am it. Do you see, you timid, scruple-mongering fool? I *am* the Universe. I, Weston, am your God and your Devil." [27]

Oh dear. It is so predictable and so egregiously wearisome. The sort of thing one might walk away from—except, alas, that it poses a genuine threat. People will believe this. Worlds will be wrecked by this. It cannot be ignored. It must be stopped. Oh, infinite tedium: now begins the grim task of fighting it.

An awful transfiguration has seized Weston at this moment, however. He has been "squatting" under a tree like a toad (Lewis has lifted the picture straight from Milton's picture of Satan in Eden, "squat like a toad", whispering in Eve's ear). But now a spasm seizes him, and he spins around and

[26] Ibid., pp. 90, 91.
[27] Ibid., p. 96.

falls to the ground, rolling and slobbering and tearing up the moss like a demoniac in the New Testament.

Weston's agenda for this planet is to try to wean the Lady away from her obedience to Maleldil. Page after page, the temptation scenes go on until we want to shout at the author, "Stop! For heaven's sake stop! Why do you prolong this part of the narrative this way? We get the point—we get the point!"

But this is an almost perfect piece of narrative art. The satanic cleverness of Weston's arguments is sickening, and then enervating, and then stultifying. Paralytic boredom grips us finally. And this is what is supposed to happen: the reader is subjected, as far as narrative can achieve it, to the very thing that Ransom is being subjected to. Weston is out to wear him down. His gambits and ploys are all a rehash for anyone who knows the story of Eden and who knows the power of vanity and discontent:

> *And He has not forbidden you to think about dwelling on the Fixed Land. . . . what might be. . . . He has never forbidden you to think about it. . . . Do you not see that He is letting go of your hand a little? . . . He is making you a full woman . . . more like the women of my world. . . . They are, as it were, little Maleldils.*[28]

We see to our horror that Weston is taking the very words of truth and giving them an opposite meaning. He tells the Lady that Ransom wishes to return to an earlier state of things, and that he fears the onward march of Maleldil's program for the universe. Ransom is bad because he "rejects the fruit he is given for the sake of the fruit he expected or

[28] Ibid., pp. 104–6.

the fruit he found last time." [29] This is the exact and true definition of evil, but Weston has invested each phrase with perverted meaning: on his accounting Ransom is rejecting the "given" fruit of this brave new world that Maleldil is offering, and is wishing for the fruit he had expected, namely everlasting subservience to Maleldil. And when the Lady asks Weston if he will teach her Death, we hear the echo, perverted, twisted, but unmistakable, of another true sentence: "Yes, it is for this that I came here, that you may have Death in abundance." [30]

This, of course, gives us one of the keys to Lewis' whole narrative art: he surprises us with what appear to be sudden and exact parallels to, even direct quotations from, our own story, the subtlety being that they arise entirely naturally from the matrix of the story he is telling, with no sense of having been borrowed from that story, or foisted upon his. The point is that what is true in one world must be true in all, so that you are going to find tempters saying the same words, or madonnas saying the same words, not because they are allegories for each other, or even quoting each other, but because each is a case in point in his own world of what is True.

Weston's appeal is all to the Lady's courage, and her sense of adventure and excitement. It is the romantic, Nietzschean appeal to one's vanity and instinct for self-dramatization. He tells her the tale of the great and courageous and venturesome Eve, and of all great and lonely and noble and rebellious women and tragic queens. It is a naked appeal to vanity, and Ransom dreads the look on her face—"like a tragic queen" as over against the "unself-conscious radiance, the

[29] Ibid., p. 114.
[30] Ibid.

frolic sanctity" that had been hers. It was "the fatal touch of invited grandeur, of enjoyed pathos—the assumption, however slight, of a role".[31] We seem to recall Milton's Satan offering Eve a mirror—and, lo and behold, Weston presently does precisely this, having dressed his Eve in the feathers of slaughtered birds. And things are getting *blurred*: the Lady is losing her grasp on "the plain intellectual bones of the problem.... Half her imagination was already filled with bright, poisonous shapes."[32]

But we notice a metamorphosis going on in the temptation itself and in Weston. It grinds down. What begins as infinitely urbane and plausible gradually becomes more flat-footed ("It is a mere command. It is forbidding for the sake of forbidding"[33]), and finally monosyllabically banal—"On the surface, great designs ... but deep within ... nothing but a black puerility".[34] Weston turns from the Lady to the task of wearing Ransom down, and his technique is simply to repeat the word "Ransom" over and over, like the dropping of water on one's head in some Oriental torture. It very nearly succeeds. Ransom gets to feeling that he has been set to "guard an imbecile or a monkey or a very nasty child.... It was fond of tearing up handfuls of turf.... It had a whole repertory of obscenities...."[35] In one horrible scene Ransom comes upon Weston gratuitously tearing the skins off some beautiful froglike creatures. Here is evil in its pointless, utterly banal, savagery. Its whole program has been destruction all along in any case, so this butchery is merely the stark exhibition of the same

[31] Ibid., p. 127.
[32] Ibid., pp. 133–34.
[33] Ibid., p. 117.
[34] Ibid., p. 123.
[35] Ibid., pp. 128, 129.

thing that was at work in the subtle suggestions about venturesomeness and growing up.

And Ransom notices that Weston now looks very much like a dead man.

> *The face which he raised from torturing the frog had that terrible power which the face of a corpse sometimes has of simply rebuffing every conceivable human attitude one can adopt towards it. The expressionless mouth, the unwinking stare of the eyes. . . . This, in fact, was not a man: . . . Weston himself was gone.*[36]

Evil had done its work. Weston had sold himself to it, like Faust; and the payment had been exacted. Nothing was left of Weston but a residue. It is the old idea of damned souls being mere shards, mere sediment.

But the thing which has looked at Ransom from Weston's face is more terrible than any mere corpse. "It did not defy goodness, it ignored it to the point of annihilation."[37] And Ransom remembers old ideas about the mere sight of the devils being one of the worst torments of hell.

> *It had seemed to him till now merely a quaint fancy. And yet (as he now saw) even the children know better: no child would have any difficulty in understanding that there might be a face the mere beholding of which was final calamity. The children, the poets, and the philosophers were right. As there is one Face above all worlds merely to see which is irrevocable joy, so at the bottom of all worlds that face is waiting whose sight alone is the misery from which none*

[36] Ibid., p. 110.
[37] Ibid.

> *who beholds it can recover. And though there seemed to be,*
> *and indeed were, a thousand roads by which a man could*
> *walk through the world, there was not a single one which*
> *did not lead sooner or later either to the Beatific or the Mis-*
> *erific Visions.*[38]

And so we have come to the third stage of the drama: what must be done. It is clear to Ransom that he himself must "do" something.

But temptation in the form of sheer weariness, doubt, self-pity, and fear assails Ransom: it's unfair; perhaps Weston is right; I won't be able to hold out; and so on and so on. Nonetheless it is perfectly clear: he himself is the key to the situation. When he finds the querulous complaint arising in his mind as to why there has been no miracle on Maleldil's side in this situation, he realizes that he himself is that miracle—a man sent across space from Thulcandra to stand in the breach. "His journey to Perelandra was not a moral exercise, nor a sham fight. If the issue lay in Maleldil's hands, Ransom and the Lady *were* those hands. The fate of a world really depended on how they behaved in the next few hours."[39] His mind races: "... the imprudence, the unfairness, the absurdity of it! Did Maleldil *want* to lose worlds? ... The preposterous truth that all really depended on their actions.... Either something or nothing must depend on individual choices."[40]

And then the bleakest of all realizations arrives: he must fight Weston physically. To his own perfervid objections that this is ridiculous, and that "a struggle with the Devil meant a *spiritual* struggle", comes the awareness that

[38] Ibid., p. 111.
[39] Ibid., p. 142.
[40] Ibid.

> *the triple distinction of truth from myth and of both from*
> *fact was purely terrestrial—was part and parcel of that unhappy*
> *division between soul and body which resulted from the Fall.*
> *Even on earth the sacraments existed as a permanent reminder*
> *that the division was neither wholesome nor final. The Incar-*
> *nation had been the beginning of its disappearance. . . . What-*
> *ever happened here would be of such a nature that earth-*
> *men would call it mythological.*[41]

The struggle, obviously, is going to have to look like those deadly struggles you get in myths—Laocoön, Perseus, Hercules. The irony is that it is only Dr. Elwin Ransom of Leicester College, Cambridge, who is doing the fighting. How inauspicious!

By this time the narrative stream has joined itself wholly with the great river into which our own Thulcandrian story flows. This drama is one incident in the larger drama which we on Earth glimpsed at Bethlehem and Jerusalem.

> *What happened on Earth, when Maleldil was born a man*
> *at Bethlehem, had altered the universe forever. . . . When*
> *Eve fell, God was not Man. He had not yet made men*
> *members of His body: since then He had, and through them*
> *henceforward He would save and suffer. One of the purposes*
> *for which He had done all this was to save Perelandra not*
> *through Himself but through Himself in Ransom.*[42]

And so Ransom must fight the Un-man, for that is what Weston is now. It is, of course, the Devil, or a devil, with whom Ransom grapples, and the sheer physical grossness of the fight, described at agonizing length, page after page,

[41] Ibid., p. 144.
[42] Ibid., pp. 144, 145.

dramatizes with terrible clarity the thing that Lewis has been working at all through his fiction: the distinction between flesh and spirit, nature and supernature, history and myth is only a provisional and contingent one. This fight does not differ *in substance* from all arguments with unbelief and apostasy and temptation. This is simply what it looks like and what it comes to when all illusions and euphemisms have been stripped away. In our own story, of course, we are familiar with this sort of thing: the same fight got down to nails, splinters, thorns, and blood.

The fight races across the face of Perelandra, with chases on fishback and more struggle, and, in a sort of ghastly and surreal pause, more endless conversation. Ransom must cope with thirst, exhaustion, and every temptation to doubt and despair ever cobbled up by hell, and the Un-man once again ticks over all the inanities of hell, droning on and on about nihilism and spiritualism and one thing and another, none of it of the slightest consequence now. It even tries whimpering and appealing to Ransom's pity.

Through it all we see a sort of epiphany of Ransom—the revelation of what he is. The peaceful scholar who no doubt thinks of himself as something of a coward because of his vivid terror at the merest thought of physical pain—this man persevering in a fight that involves being torn with the fingernails of a demon, pursuing the fight beyond exhaustion and beyond hope. At what seems the final point, when it looks as though the two of them are to be dashed on the rocks by the surf and Weston cries out in terror, we see the plain, decent, schooled Ransom calling out to his fellow in danger (after all, Weston is a fellow-creature, and the two of them are "together" in this final peril, in a sudden and dramatic switch), "Are you there, Weston? What cheer? Pull yourself together. All that stuff you've been talking is lunacy. Say a child's prayer if you can't say a man's. Repent your sins. Take my hand."[43] All these flat platitudes from the playing fields and common rooms of the schools and from superstitious nannies and vicars—that is what it comes down to in the crunch, and in that crunch we see the luminous truth and force of what all those platitudes were really about.

The fight descends to the lower parts of the Earth, underwater, down to fiery subterranean chasms. ("Buried with him by baptism into death. . . . He descended into hell"—we keep hearing these echoes.) One horror—or apparent horror—attends the last struggle and end of the Un-man, when Ransom finally smashes him and tips what is left of him, or it, into the fiery abyss. A nightmarish creature like a gigantic crustacean has crawled up out of a hole and seems to be coming for Ransom. Well, he thinks, this is the end. They've summoned help from all the horrors there are. But, as he pauses after having delivered the final blow to the Un-man, Ransom realizes that the creature has nothing at all to do with this struggle, and is simply going on its way. Why, he wonders, should one "quarrel with an animal for having more legs or eyes than oneself?"[44]

This is one of three points in these final scenes when we catch glimpses of creatures who are beautiful or fascinating or awesome, but who clearly are no part of the story. At one point, floating exhausted on his fish after part of the chase, Ransom sees a humanlike face under the water, "and he guessed that the creature's reaction to him was the very same as his to it—an uneasy, though not hostile, bewilderment. Each was wholly irrelevant to the other. They met as

[43] Ibid., p. 171.
[44] Ibid., p. 182.

the branches of different trees meet when the wind brings them together." [45] The other point occurs when Ransom is on his way up from his ordeal in the underworld. He looks down "through fathom below fathom of shafts and natural arches" and sees, on a smooth floor at an infinite distance, a sort of chariot being drawn by four beetlelike creatures, and, in the chariot, a great mantled form, "huge and still and slender". The whole procession moves past "with insufferable majesty and went out of sight. Assuredly the inside of this world was not for man. But it was for something." [46]

Why these bits and flecks on the screen? Cannot Lewis stay with his story? Must we have these distractions? The answer is that all this is crucial to this particular kind of story. The very pattern of the drama requires that we never forget for long that, awesome and gripping as it is, it is only one of many stories which may or may not touch each other, but which eventually all form parts of the Whole Pattern. This is one of the prime characteristics of myth, and, it seems, of our own story. Who are the Magi? Who are the seraphim? Who is Melchizedek? What about the fight between Saint Michael the Archangel and Satan for the body of Moses? We don't know much. The story doesn't tell us. They cross the stage in a moment and go on their way. When will the lines converge? Well, we keep on . . .

With Ransom's emergence back up into the clear light and air, the narrative itself rises to an almost wholly visionary level. Ransom's emergence itself has been accomplished by his feet slipping on clay and his finding himself being borne along in deep, swift-flowing water. In a sort of death-like baptism, he is swallowed up and delivered out into the

[45] Ibid., p. 161.
[46] Ibid., p. 183.

broad daylight. It is his sabbath. All is still and ecstatic. Running water, fruit, a strange song in the air, pellucid clarity, a climb up a great mountain where he discovers that "to be always climbing this was not, in his present mood, a process but a state, and in that state of life he was content"—this is what he finds. In a final, small, and incredible act of courtesy to Weston himself, he erects and engraves a memorial stone, phrasing carefully and without judgment what Weston's achievements were, and what had happened to him ("he gave up his will and reason to the Bent Eldil").

The fabric and the pattern of the last scene are so intricately woven that we find ourselves obliged to acknowledge the obvious: this pageant with its insupportably dazzling, almost remorseless, sequences, all charged with paradoxes, mysteries, riddles, imponderables, and glories—there is no way other than this pageant itself of saying *quite this*. And when we have said this, we have of course said the thing that applies to any good artistic achievement. The Venus of Milo, for example: there are endless ways of diagramming or hymning feminine beauty, but there is no other sculpture which does exactly this. Or *The Divine Comedy*: thousands of books have been written about hell, purgatory, and paradise, but there is no other poem which does exactly what this one does, nor any way other than poetry of achieving exactly this. This is not to claim for Lewis' achievement in *Perelandra* a dignity or success equal to that sculptor's or Dante's: it is simply to reiterate the obvious, that no explication can do what art does. Or put it another way: you have to reach for music or ceremony or poetry or heraldry in order to catch as much of the *brightness* of the ineffable as human imagination can catch. Ratiocination and expository prose (metaphysics, say, or moral theology) can plot out things, like a map, and there are times when what we need is a map; but the "truth" of a map differs from the "truth" of a stage set or a painting. A map is rarely awesome, and if the very thing you want to achieve is to suggest something about the awesome properties of the Alps, say, you are going to have to give us something other than thin brown contour lines.

The thing which we find in this pageant which forms the denouement of the whole drama is a pattern in which the rock ribs of sheer truth form the structure which supports the scarlet and gold fabric of glory. Seen in this light, fact *is* glorious. Truth is blissful. Reality is hilarious. Speculation and ratiocination and hard intellectual work find themselves transfigured and rising on wings of awe and adoration. It is all very far from being an escape from reality into blur and vapor and illusion and hallucination. It is the unfurling of the concrete actuality of which all mathematics and physics and logic and ethics and astronomy and theology speak. We see, in a word, the Dance.

How do you speak of a dance? It is one thing to list the necessary motions: hold your partner's right hand that way; put your left foot there; now turn thus; and so forth. It is another to see the gilded ballroom in Vienna with a thousand glittering nobles and their ladies dancing to the music of Strauss, and still another thing to *be* one of the dancers. A list of the motions and figures in this Dance which culminates this drama, and toward which the whole drama has been straining, would begin something like this: the two *eldila*, Malacandra and Perelandra themselves, appear, simultaneously speeding and motionless, towering, noble, hardly able to find a mode of presenting themselves which the mortal eyes of Ransom can bear; they speak of mystery upon mystery with Ransom, Perelandra touching on her own past suzerainty in this planet and of her joyous task on this birth-day of this new world, of handing over that suzerainty to the King and Queen who are the true heirs and sovereigns here; Malacandra, or Mars, appears as something like ultimate masculinity—like rhythm and quantity, with a spear in his hand—and Perelandra, or Venus, appears as something like ultimate femininity—like melody and quality, with an open hand; Ransom recognizes charity here: "pure, spiritual, intellectual love shot from their faces like barbed lightning";[47] he sees what gender (as opposed to sex) means, and what mythology is ("gleams of celestial strength and beauty falling on a jungle of filth and imbecility"[48]); at the solemn ceremony which presently arranges itself, Ransom breaks in, like Saint Peter at the Transfiguration, with some banality, and is properly hushed; the purpose of the prohibition on the Fixed Land is disclosed; and then—and then—with pure light filling the scene "like wine in a bowl", the climax is reached: "the holy thing, Paradise itself in its two Persons", appears, "and the gods kneeled and bowed their huge bodies before the small forms of that young King and Queen."[49]

But that is only the beginning of the steps in the Dance. In Ransom's questions to Tor, the King, and then in the great hymn whose refrain, over and over, is "Blessed be He!" we find myth, theology, metaphysics, and poetry becoming indistinguishable. On and on it goes, riddle upon riddle unraveled, mystery upon mystery evoked, splendor upon splendor accumulated.

It is a daunting thing which Lewis has attempted in this narrative, but we may see in it at least one of the possibilities of narrative art—one which has lain fallow for some centuries now, and which may have been worth reviving.

[47] Ibid., p. 200.
[48] Ibid., p. 201.
[49] Ibid., p. 204.

CHAPTER FIVE

That Hideous Strength:
The Miserific Vision

A close commentary on *That Hideous Strength* could easily run to thousands of pages, since we have here a kind of narrative analogous to the visionary novels of George Mac-Donald and Charles Williams. The most obvious effect of this sort of narrative on the prose itself is that it is possible to "unpack" every phrase and to discover therein themes and images that all open out onto the gigantic vista lying around the borders of the small part of the tale that forms the immediate drama in the book itself. Put another way, the narrative is closer in its texture to poetry or to pageant than it is to the prose that we are accustomed to meet in novels. You can creep line by line through a poem—say *The Faerie Queene* or *Paradise Lost* or *Four Quartets*—and the work will sustain and reward this line-by-line scrutiny, even if the reader of your commentary cannot sustain it. The point here is that we *expect* extreme economy, even density, in poetry; we know that the language, image by image, sound by sound, word by word, represents the purest possible product of the fiercest refining heat that the poet's imagination can bring to bear on his materials. To try to say exactly what Spenser or Milton or Eliot have said in their poems, the critic must run to thousands of words, and when he has finished he must send the reader back to the poem itself with the confession that his commentary is about as close to the poet's achievement as is a contour map to the Alps.

This is true of all good prose narrative as well. It is not as though we may say that Spenser has to refine his materials while Tolstoy or James may load theirs up with alloy and dross. There is, presumably, no epaulette in Tolstoy and no tassel in James that is there at a mere hap. It is extremely difficult to chase down just what the final difference *is* between poetry and prose: but we may say lamely that in the common run of things any given page of James will not invite as many lines of explication as will a page of Eliot. That is perhaps a misleading way of putting it, since you can write as fat a book about Isabel Archer as you can about Prufrock—but remember that Isabel Archer has three hundred pages to herself and Prufrock has only five.

Lewis' narratives, especially when we come to *That Hideous Strength* and *Till We Have Faces*, seem to wrench the category "prose" about. If you are the sort who annotates what you read, you will find that a page of this prose requires more underlinings and more "Aha's" in the margin and more asterisks leading to excited footnotes and more cross-references, than does the average page of James or Tolstoy. (Once more I adduce these two novelists, not because I wish to set Lewis in their company as novelists, but because they supply us with a sort of touchstone when we are speaking of the art of prose narrative. It is often useful to keep referring to a Rembrandt or a Mozart or a Tolstoy when you are talking of a given art form, just to keep an undoubted standard in view.) This is not because James and Tolstoy have less to say, or that a given page of their prose is less interesting, but simply because that *kind* of narrative does not exhibit a phrase-by-phrase or image-by-image complexity in its pattern.

We may find another analogy for the distinction that is being drawn here by recalling the difference between pageant and drama. In the former you have, usually, a rather complex but nonetheless obvious array of elements each of which is fairly simple in itself, the pattern deriving from the juxtaposition and intermingling of these elements, a bit like mosaic. Costume, music, spectacle, speech, movement—they are all easy to see, and whatever drama there is at stake turns out to be a sort of sum of these colorful elements. In ordinary drama you may have all of these elements—indeed you do have them all—but the manner in which the playwright mingles them for his pattern demands fewer visible *seams*, we might say. There is nothing wrong with seams, heaven knows, in brocade or mosaic or pageant; the seams themselves are an acknowledged part of the integrity of the whole. But there are other ways of getting a pattern—tapestry, say, or fresco—where you don't want the elements to be so visible. We might think of the various versions of the Faust story here: Marlowe works it up after one fashion, and Goethe after another, and Gounod yet another. We cannot quite test one by the others, complaining for example that Goethe's work is more subtle than Gounod's because he does not depend for the force of his drama upon our actually hearing Marguerite shriek, whereas Gounod does. The reply to this, of course, is that Gounod's art depends on *noises*.

So the obvious question here is, Well, then, why adduce Tolstoy and James at all? And the reply would have to run something like this: because these artists are the ones we think of when we think of prolonged prose narrative in the modern world, and that is certainly the category in which Lewis' adult fiction falls. If we wish to run things down a bit more closely and ask whether we are speaking of the *novel*, then we must demur, at least for the moment. Lewis is patently working in obedience to canons that do not seem to fit easily into the category "novel" as it is commonly spoken of by contemporary criticism. But our task is not so much to find a category for Lewis' work as to see what the nature of his achievement is. How does his art relate to human experience? Does it throw light on that experience, or obscure it? Does it enrich or blight our capacity to appreciate experience? Does it ennoble or trivialize our vision of man? Has the artist handled his materials skillfully? These are some of the questions we want to ask of any art.

The visible components of the action in *That Hideous Strength* are these: the marriage of Mark and Jane Studdock, Bracton College and its affairs, Belbury, St. Anne's, and Merlin. It is exciting enough to chase any or all of these elements through the narrative without ever bothering to ask what really controls the drama. But if we are pretending to come at what an artist has done, we must do more than exclaim over this or that bit in his achievement that may momentarily excite us—this glint of gold on the helmet in a Rembrandt, or that high E-flat in Verdi, or the clerestory arches at Norwich. What is the *whole* thing about?

There are two ways of coming at the task of making some comment on Lewis' achievement in *That Hideous Strength*. The more natural approach, which has the advantage of fidelity to the narrative *qua* narrative, is simply to move into the story line by line and scene by scene, remarking on how this action or that aside or the other image builds up the pattern which we will find spread out in front of us by the time we reach the end. The disadvantage to this method is that the commentary will be many times longer than the book itself. The other method is to amass observations on how the various components of the action are presented to us, and then to attempt to descry the pattern of the whole. The advantage to this is that it enables us to bring together information from all parts of the book; the disadvantage of course is that it treats the material as though it is, precisely, "information", and that does not do justice to the development of the narrative. But because this narrative is so like poetry in its density and its complex and interwoven allusiveness, we may adopt the latter scheme, at least for the moment.

Lewis took his title from a sixteenth-century poem by the Scottish poet Sir David Lyndsay, who was, among other things, the Lyon king of arms, that is, the chief herald of Scotland. That itself may give us a clue as to how to read this and all of Lewis' fiction; there is a sense in which it is all heraldic. The images, as in heraldry, are all utterly stark. The poem from which Lewis took his title is "Ane dialog betwix Experience and ane Courtier of the miserabill estait of the World". The lines involved are these: "The shadow of that hyddeous strength / Sax myle and more it is of length." The hideous strength is the Tower of Babel.

Here, perhaps, is our first key to the drama. Babel. Chaos. Disintegration. And what was the particular nature of the disintegration at Babel? Was it not the breaking apart of language—say a breakdown between words and meaning, or the loss of the ability to attach intelligible meaning to things, a curse visited upon the race answering to its sin of *hubris*? We will erect a tower reaching to heaven. No, you will not (say the gods), for here is what will happen when you try to do this. Confusion. The connection of all this with the action in *That Hideous Strength* is that what starts out as an attempt on the part of the "Progressive Element" in Bracton College to build a tower to heaven, ends up in a scene indistinguishable from Babel. We have a hint as to the sort of imagery Lewis is prepared to use here when we learn that the building which is to house the staff of the National Institute for Coordinated Experiments (the N.I.C.E.) "was one which would make a quite noticeable addition to the skyline of New York".[1] Apparently it is to reach to heaven. We also learn that the enterprise to be undertaken by this N.I.C.E. is nothing less nor other than the recasting, nay, the re-creating, of English life, and eventually of human existence itself.

But it is Jane whom we meet first. She is alone and musing in the flat which she and her husband Mark Studdock occupy in Edgestow, the small university town where Mark holds a fellowship in sociology at Bracton College, a small college like All Souls, in that it has only fellows and no undergraduates. We find that Jane is musing about the topic of marriage—indeed, "matrimony" is the first word in the book. The words which are running through her head are from the marriage rite in the *Book of Common Prayer*: "Matrimony was ordained, thirdly, for the mutual society, help, and comfort that the one ought to have of the other."

There is the central theme of the book. For if marriage is the place where we find the idea of Charity guarded and taught and enacted, and if Charity is the very nature of our freedom and joy—if it is the very pattern of the Dance—then every element in this book is arrayed around that center.

---

[1] C. S. Lewis, *That Hideous Strength* (New York: Macmillan Publishing Company, 1965), p. 23.

Take Bracton College and its affairs, for example. In the meetings of the fellows and in their private conversations, we discover a murderous cynicism and a cavalier contempt for all traditional sentiment. It is impossible, for example, for Mark to discover exactly who among these scheming fellows constitutes the Inner Ring, to which he would gladly sell his soul to gain entry. Every syllable of his conversation with any of them, and every waking thought, is thrall to the one tyrannous fear that he might not be allowed *in*. He attaches himself, brightly, hopefully, pitiably, and, he hopes, insouciantly, to one after the other of these cads, hoping against hope that he may have finally found the right one. The bleak discovery that he eventually makes at Belbury is that there is no center at all. The entire enterprise is a shifting, sinister kaleidoscope of perfidy. It is all a ghastly parody of the mutuality, trust, obedience, and joy at work in Charity, of which matrimony is the great case in point, or sacrament. (Mark's marriage to Jane is something of an irritant and a bore, though.)

Further, in these college meetings we find that all sentiment is mocked. The proposal before the fellows is that they consider selling the ancient wood, Bragdon, which stands deep and silent and walled inside the college grounds, at the far end of one's progress through the quads and the bowling green. When it comes down to it, the only argument for keeping the wood is a sentimental one: wouldn't it be a pity to cut down and clear away all those noble and ancient trees? Old Canon Jewel, one of the fellows, tries feebly to put the case for this, but of course he is just a superannuated old fool who still attaches weight to such things as tradition and sentiment, so he is overridden. What sort of bite has this line of thought over against the force of sheer progress? We will see more of this presently.

As the action moves along, however, this college business that seems so routine and normal (oh, there's always a certain amount of minor intrigue in small faculties, ho-ho) thickens and hardens into Belbury, that paradigm of hell itself. We see nothing at all at Belbury, the country house purchased and occupied by N.I.C.E., whose seeds were not carefully planted and watered in the Common Room at Bracton.

Closer in to the nerve but also in contrast to the order of Charity, we see Jane. It is not that Jane has set herself against Charity, or at least not consciously. Indeed, our sympathies are very much with her. She is an intelligent, capable, articulate, university-educated woman who finds herself trapped in the very small cell of a marriage that has dwindled to almost nothing. There she is, in her flat day after day, supposed to be finding fulfillment as a wife and housekeeper, with a husband whose mind and imagination are entirely preoccupied with career and college business and his cronies on the faculty. What is a woman to do? Is it really the case that a woman's whole business in life is to wait in silence at home, day after day, for whatever tag ends of attention a rather tiresome young husband may vouchsafe her from time to time?

Ironically we find that Jane is working on a doctoral thesis on Donne—on his "triumphant vindication of the body". Donne's poetry and prose *Devotions* are, of course, shot through with the lively awareness that the flesh is the very mediator of meaning to us mortals, and Jane apparently finds this idea intriguing. As it turns out, alas, not only is there very little in the way of the physical between her and Mark: she herself is vexed by being typecast as a "woman", with all its paraphernalia of nattering in kitchens and shopping and hats and so forth, when what she really wants is to be thought of as an intellectual. She would like the dignity of being a *mind*. Even her clothes ought to fit this image, she feels: "She liked her clothes to be rather severe and in colours that were really good on serious aesthetic grounds—clothes which would make it plain to everyone that she was an intelligent adult and not a woman of the chocolate-box variety. . . ." [2]

All this is plausible and harmless enough, heaven knows. The only trouble is that the drama in this tale happens to disclose for us the diabolical horrors that stand at the far end of the disjuncture of mind and body—of gnosticism, say. That very old and popular and persistent idea that the division between spirit and flesh is a division between worthy and worthless—we see it in Jane's struggle to detach herself from the vexing business of being a "mere" woman, and in the marriage of Jane and Mark where the idea of matrimony is no longer clothed with the plain, daily business of being truly man and wife to each other, and we see it reaching chaotic fruition in the breakdown of language at the final banquet at Belbury, where meaning has finally departed altogether from the "flesh" of words that ought to clothe it, and in the disembodied Head, which dribbles and drools inanely at the center of the operation there, and to which they all pay ghastly homage. You cannot, in the interest of pure intellect, disavow the body, for all of its plumbing and embarrassing fleshliness. In our human and mortal realm here, words without meaning, idea without action, mind without body all turn out to be chaos.

It is not that Lewis wishes to imply that Jane should abandon all her intellectual aspirations and settle back down to being a woman, with "woman" entailing nothing more than

[2] Ibid., p. 28.

housework and hats. Housework is certainly a universal image of the domestic service that has attached itself to femininity in all tribes and civilizations from the beginning; but that domestic service itself seems only to hint at something of which femininity is the custodian in this mortal life, perhaps because there is a quality like this in the very fabric of Creation, say, that answers in its significance to the *other* quality, masculinity. This way of looking at things is all unfurled in the vision of Mars and Venus in *Perelandra*, of course.

In so small a detail as hats, for example, we may see a mere hint of all this. Periodically we find Jane putting on her hat, or thinking about buying one. It would be carrying the search for symbols to grotesque lengths to urge that hats appear in this tale trailing some great clouds of significance. On the other hand, what is implicit here and in all of Lewis' vision is the notion that it may at least be worth pausing momentarily in the presence of some oddity as ancient and universal as a head covering for women. Lewis would not, I think, argue that women ought to keep their hats on (although he was writing this in the 1940s, when most women put on a hat even to go shopping). He would, however, be mildly curious as to what it all might mean: was there a mythic and protohistoric notion of some mystery and glory attaching to femininity that might be worth veiling, as we veil or protect all supremely fine things? It might be so; but whether it is or not, and whether hats represent some sort of detritus from that mythic deposit, no one can say; and in any case it would be impossible to go back to that sort of thing; it would be like insisting that we begin setting up altars at every railroad junction since crossroads used to be thought significant.

Jane and Mark form the nexus, so to speak, which ties the various elements of the action together. Bracton College comes home to Jane, as it were, in the person of Mark; or put it the other way: their domestic situation opens out via Mark in the one direction toward Bracton College (and thence to Belbury), and via Jane in the other direction (toward the household at St. Anne's). And Merlin stands in the breach as a great potentiality, the alarming thing being that his enormous powers may be pressed into the service of either antagonist in the final struggle. The drama entails nothing more nor less nor other than chaos versus order. Ennui versus joy. Impotence versus strength. Sterility versus fecundity. Cruelty versus mercy. Blur versus clarity. Cynicism versus fidelity. Hell, in a word, versus paradise.

Myth and poetry, and mediaeval theology and vision, furnish us with a thousand variations on the theme, and Lewis set himself the task of dramatizing it all in local terms: a marriage, a career, a small college, a political experiment. That is all plain sailing for criticism: here is fiction attempting to see life steadily and see it whole, as Matthew Arnold thinks literary art should do. But Merlin? That is a rupture in the fabric.

In order to place Merlin in the pattern and see the point, we must follow the action. It leads toward Merlin. Or let us say rather that it asks for Merlin at such and such a point, the way the action in *Macbeth* asks for Banquo's ghost, or the action in *The Tempest* asks for the laying down of Prospero's powers.

We find, returning to Jane, that she is hagridden with dreams. She seems to have a sort of clairvoyance in which she will dream a thing and presently see it in the external world. This occurs early in the action, where she dreams of a face. We may see something of the density of imagery at work in Lewis' narrative by noting the long paragraph in chapter 1 in which this occurs. This is characteristic of the narrative technique at work throughout the story. Almost everything may be annotated, as it were, or at least seems to tease us with possible analogies, all the while pursuing its serene way through the action.

For one thing, it runs like a motif through all of Lewis' fiction that women see things more clearly than men. Lucy, Mrs. Beaver, Jane, Mother Dimble, Psyche—they seem to have a capacity which is at one and the same time earthy, practical, and commonsensical, and also clairvoyant, or at least specially sensitive and perspicacious. Where everyone else muddles about with blinders on, these women again and again seem to see straight through to the point. We may observe Jane later in this narrative instinctively distrusting the cad Feverstone to whom Mark toadies, and seeing the all-important Curry as a pompous fool, "and Mark a fool for being impressed by him".

This capacity which exhibits itself in these women is not an allegory for anything at all, it seems to me. Rather, it is a natural case in point of something that is hinted at in other stories. In the myth, it is Psyche, the soul (which in Greek is feminine), who sees the god; in another ancient story it is the woman who, unlike the prophets and patriarchs and kings who merely bear witness *to* the Word, herself bears the Word, in her womb. She has in her very anatomy a place, a home, that receives and nourishes what is true. Mere fancy, of course—but fancy that haunts the borders of myth, Gospel, and everyday biological and psychological experience.

We may also note in this scene the appearance of the face which Jane sees. It is "foreign-looking, bearded and rather yellow, with a hooked nose". Its name turns out to be Alcasan. We may, if we choose, suppose that it is the face of an Arab, whose characteristic religion would be Islam, which denies the Incarnation, that scandalous union of the divine and the human in real flesh. Here we have, not Lewis writing a curse over the Arabs (we discover later that it is the head of "a Saracen"), but rather the image of a certain notion. And it is a notion very much to the purpose of the drama here, since it will be very much by the plain flesh of Jane herself that godhood (read Charity) will be mediated to Mark. Mark's salvation comes not by his being argued out of his fatuousness but by the memory and the reality of Jane. (We may even, if we wish, suppose that Lewis did not ignore the commonplace "plain Jane" when he chose her name: she, like Mary, say, is nobody particular. Not Berengaria, or Clothilde, or Hildeburgh; just Jane.)

Further, we find that this face, or head, as it seems to be, is addressed by a good-looking man with pince-nez and a pointed beard. His name is Frost, and as it happens, before the action has gone very far we find that he is chilling indeed. But beyond this we find ourselves teased by the following speculation (to which Lewis gives not one nod of encouragement): Frost is a one-syllable, five-letter name beginning with the letter F; there is another figure familiar to all of us moderns whose name fits that description, and whose face looks like Frost's. And it will be remarked that Frost treats Alcasan as a sort of patient/prisoner, and, in a horrible moment in Jane's dream, twists Alcasan's head *off*. He manipulates heads, apparently, separating them from all the plain and obvious plumbing that makes up bodies. If we do not choose to hear the echo "Freud" here, we need not. The story remains the same, and no allegory is necessary.

Then there occurs one of those metamorphoses common in dreams. The head now appears "with a flowing white beard all covered with earth. It belonged to an old man whom some people were digging up in a kind of churchyard—a sort of ancient British, druidical kind of man, in a long mantle." Janes sees that he is waking up, and cries out warnings to the people digging him up. But he sits up and begins talking in something like Spanish.

This is fair enough matter for dreams. The difficulty is that we see all this later—not just in the emergence of Merlin into the action, speaking as it were a sort of "Celticized Latin", which would signal his primitive Celt-hood baptized by Christianity, but far more than that, in the moral implication of the whole effort of the N.I.C.E. to root out from life and stamp on all that is noble and grave and mysterious—all, in a word, that is buried (or planted, say) in tradition and that nourishes the roots of civilized life.

What happens, if the dream is true, is that if you tinker about with things the way Frost does with Alcasan, treating them as mere data, deracinating them, and introducing a fissure between head and body (that is, form and content, or mind and matter, or theory and plain actuality)—if you do that, which gnosticism does, you may awaken and unloose things that you hadn't quite anticipated. What you thought was data might loom suddenly upon you. Merlin might start up out of his coffin.

If this seems mere trivia and spookiness, we may observe our own epoch: we tinker with the subconscious and unleash universal illness and perplexity; we fiddle with the atom and bring the Cloud over our heads; we pillage the earth and find ourselves without fuel; we wrench the finely tuned ecological balance that seems to obtain in Nature and find ourselves poisoned, polluted, starved; we dragoon the airwaves in the interest of mass and instant information and turn the world into a global village where predatory passions are no longer separated from each other by sheer distance, and we discover that we cannot run a village of that size.

This is to go very far afield from Jane's dream and from Lewis' narrative. But the whole point in the drama here is that what we can see going on in Edgestow and its environs is also at work all through the fabric of human existence. It is not a diverting web of allegories that Lewis has spun here: rather it is narrative in whose warp and woof we see threads we recognize, woven into a smallish pattern that seems to answer to the big one all around us. Or, to change the metaphor, it may be a case in point of the poet perceiving the fear in the handful of dust: Lewis seeing in these rather inconsequential events in a provincial backwater the damnation that grins at us from the whole horizon.

There follows a scene in which we watch the machinations of the Progressive Element, which is scheming to bring about really apocalyptic turns of events under the modest guise of parliamentary procedure, small print, euphemism, and unobtrusive manipulating of attitudes in a committee meeting. Meanwhile we find Jane visiting the Dimbles. It is an uncomfortable time of self-revelation for Jane. Upstairs with Mother Dimble "(one tended to call her Mother Dimble)" [3] there is some "strictly feminine" conversation which Jane, trying to maintain a slightly superior detachment, finds indefinably comforting. Then, with Mother Dimble's sudden question as to whether she is all right, Jane breaks down and cries. "And then, for a moment, Mrs. Dimble became simply a grown-up as grown-ups had been when one was a very small child: large, warm, soft objects to whom one ran with bruised knees or broken toys." [4] One sometimes remembered occasions like this which had seemed "an insult to one's maturity; now, for the moment, she was back in those forgotten, yet infrequent, times when fear or misery induced

[3] Ibid., p. 29.
[4] Ibid., p. 30.

a willing surrender and surrender brought comfort. Not to detest being petted and pawed was contrary to her whole theory of life".[5]

Later, when Jane is trying to regain her wonted self-possession, she exclaims, "Damn the Dimbles!"[6] And, in an early conversation with Grace Ironwood at St. Anne's, we find her speaking of this clairvoyant power with which she is saddled: "But I don't *want* it.... I want to lead an ordinary life. I want to do my own work. It's unbearable! Why should I be selected for this horrible thing?"[7]

There, in a word, is the trouble. Jane finds that she is being interfered with. This is the last thing she wants. What she wants is independence, self-determination, dignity, and so forth; and here she finds herself being dragged into some absurd broil that takes her right out of whatever life she might have forged for herself.

St. Anne's is the place where this interference takes place, and it is the place of Jane's salvation. It may be noted that in Western hagiology, Saint Anne is the mother of the Mother of God. Lewis was aware of this, of course, and, given the particular iconography at work in his story here, this is appropriate. Jane becomes, as it were, the *theotokos*, the "God-bearer" to Mark, since it is by means of her flesh that salvation is mediated to him. He must be salvaged ("saved") from the gnostic trash heap which is his life now— that life that knows only vacant, generalized, abstract, sociological categories, and nothing of real flesh-and-blood human beings. Once, for example, on a visit to the nearby village of Cure Hardy with his Progressive Element colleague Cosser, we see Mark vaguely haunted by the fugitive thought

[5] Ibid.
[6] Ibid., p. 45.
[7] Ibid., p. 66.

that real working men in a pub with real beer and thick sandwiches are somehow closer to the truth of the matter than his own sociological generalizations about "the working class" and certainly than this bore Cosser here. But it does not lodge in Mark's consciousness: ". . . his education has had the curious effect of making things that he read and wrote more real to him than things he saw. Statistics about agricultural labourers were the substance; any real ditcher, ploughman, or farmer's boy was the shadow."[8] In his peril and near-damnation at Belbury, it is the memory of the flesh-and-blood Jane that keeps returning him to his senses; and in an unabashedly erotic closing scene, it is to that Jane that he is returned, chastened, purged, and now a catechumen in the school of Charity.

The household at St. Anne's becomes the mother of Charity to Jane. Here she is bundled into a rather dumpy collection of odd types, and here she finds herself head-over-heels in the very things that she has wished to avoid. For example, she has thought of herself as enlightened and liberal in her politics, but when it comes down to it, she finds it odd that there should be such a workaday *equality* assumed here, where Ivy Maggs, the charwoman, seems to enjoy a place quite as secure and dignified as Jane's or anybody else's. There is even a bear (Mr. Bultitude) who lumbers about, obviously entirely at home. But on the other hand, there is clearly some vexing notion of obedience in the air, too, which is a bore, since what Jane wishes from life is independence and self-determination. It is quite clear that Ransom is at the head of the household.

St. Anne's is a case in point of the same thing that has been imagined, especially in the Arthurian poetry of Charles

[8] Ibid., p. 87.

Williams, to have been at work in Logres, which is Arthurian Britain. In Logres there was made the great experiment in Charity, namely the Round Table, where the knights would place themselves and their powers at the service not of conquest but of good works. It was all to have been carried on under the kingship of Arthur; but of course it all broke up in adultery, cupidity, and the perfidy of Mordred; and what might have been paradise was doomed to drain out sadly into mere history, like the doom that came upon that other brief and blissful place, Eden.

Ransom, who makes his final appearance now in this third book of the trilogy, is the Pendragon of Logres—the office first held by Uther and then Arthur. Camilla Denniston explains this to Jane: "And he is the Pendragon of Logres. This house, all of us here, and Mr. Bultitude and Pinch, are all that's left of the Logres: all the rest has become merely Britain."[9] That is, here is a realm (only one household now) where things are ordered according to the hierarchy of Charity, which throws all of our notions of either democracy or tyranny into a cocked hat. It is more egalitarian than democracy ever dreams of being, and more absolutist than the most serene tyranny. What saves it from politics is that, quite simply, Charity rules here, as it does in the City of God which is the pattern from which all patterns derive, in matrimony, in good families and religious houses, and in good kingdoms. Ransom is the "Fisher King" also, who, in the Arthurian stories, was the Keeper of the Hallows (the Spear and the Grail). Here at St. Anne's he is custodian of the most sacred trust, namely, the order of Charity. Jane is invited by Denniston to come and meet Ransom. "He is really a Head, you see. We have all agreed to

[9] Ibid., p. 195.

take his orders." [10] There is no escaping the word "Head" there: at the center of St. Anne's there is a real Head, doing what a head should do, namely ruling the body in wisdom and charity. At Belbury we will find the ghastly counterfeit of this, with a Head to be sure, but one that is a dribbling inanity, at the center. That Head has been severed from its body by the gnostic hatred of the physical, in the interest of the purely intellectual, just as the head (Mark) in the marriage of Mark and Jane has been severed from the body (Jane).

The company which we find at St. Anne's constitutes a sort of paradigm of Charity. Not that each one of them exhibits any extraordinary sanctity: far from it. The overwhelming impression, in so far as anything so inauspicious as the household at St. Anne's can be said to be overwhelming, is of plainness and ordinariness. This is of the quintessence of Lewis' tales: on the one hand cups of tea and cakes and ducks and pints of bitter; and on the other the arcane, the bizarre, the grotesque, the bestial, and finally the diabolical. St. Anne's is most emphatically ordinary, we might say. It is not a collection of intellectuals, or of saints, or of aristocrats, or of "bright young things", or of "clever people", or of any other exclusive and fascinating elite. Its population appears to be quite random, and it is certainly ordinary. Here, in the common run and routine of conventional household life and minor responsibilities in the kitchen and the garden, and in the courtesies that assist and guard the intercourse of one person with another—here in all this platitudinous, shopworn ordinariness we find the jewel Charity. The picture here is very far from the sort of thing at work in various visionary experiments in Life

[10] Ibid., p. 116.

Together attempted at such places as Brook Farm and so forth. There is no hint of the rather fevered and solemn self-consciousness that seemed to animate those efforts at utopia. If this tale were more strictly allegorical, we could not avoid identifying St. Anne's and the Church. But for purposes of this tale, we find not an allegory so much as a believable case in point of the sort of life that is taught and attempted in the Church.

The plainness at St. Anne's stands starkly over against the grotesquery at Belbury, and we see played out in these two contrasting households everything that Lewis wrote about so often: on the one hand, good health and normality and humility and loyalty and merriment and candor and courtesy; and on the other, disease and cruelty and treachery and mockery and apostasy and the unnatural, all carried on under the self-congratulatory assumption that we are the "thoughtful people" and that this is progress and enlightenment.

Lewis rang the changes on this in his essays. He called himself an "Old Western Man", even a dinosaur, making no secret that he dreaded with mortal dread the moral forces that would uproot us all from the unexciting virtues that are guarded and perpetuated in such platitudinous conventions as civility and "stock responses". Give me any day, he says in effect, the Cockney cabbie who, without ever having studied the *Nichomachean Ethics*, reacts with horror or disgust in the face of the horrible and the disgusting, rather than the cynical university don who, having read his Aristotle, looks at *all* ethical imperatives with amused and avuncular detachment. Give me any day the heathen wringing a chicken's neck in front of a totem rather than the anthropologist who looks at all notions of expiation as quaint and suggestive data. The point, of course, is not cabbies versus dons, or heathens versus anthropologists: rather it is between the man who suspects that something real, even awe-ful, is mediated to us in these universal conventions of civility and these taboos, and the man who, acknowledging no such thing, has set out to remake it all.

At St. Anne's we meet the black-clad spinster Grace Ironwood. Jane is brought to her after having been admitted at a narrow side gate—a strait gate and narrow way, if we wish to hear this language. Grace's function is to bring Jane to Ransom. In the pageantlike scenario in which we find the drama in this tale occurring, we might have supposed that a figure named Grace would be all smiles and affability. But it is not always so, certainly not for Jane. Her entry into the household of Charity seems dismal to her, since it is clearly going to involve the jettisoning of virtually everything she has tried so hard to preserve: independence, dignity, and so forth. And we may also note Miss Ironwood's surname. Lewis, who knew his old English poetry and his Latin hymnody, knew that the Cross has been called "sweetest wood and sweetest iron". Those rough and unlikely instruments of discomfort are lauded as sweet, according to one vision of things. The way *in* may involve—nay, *does* involve—a crucifixion, as Lewis well knew from his own unwilling conversion.

And we also meet Dr. Dimble, a professor at Northumberland College which, like Mark's Bracton, is part of the University of Edgestow. He is a plain man who knows all about the history of language and the Arthurian stories. He is a good husband and a kind man, but we see in him the capacity to be outraged: when Mark, the unspeakably groveling lackey of Belbury, tries to insist that Dimble should have told him about the mistreatment of Jane by Belbury, Dr. Dimble says merely, "*You?*" And then Lewis relates, "For one moment, the first for many years, Mark saw himself exactly as a man like Dimble saw him. It almost took his breath away." [11] Here is the point at which goodness is no longer kind to evil. Here is the whip of thongs driving the money-changers out of the temple. But Dr. Dimble, being human, must struggle with a lack of charity toward Mark, and we watch that struggle. The self-examination to which he subjects himself is the struggle of charity with self-righteousness. "Did I give way to my temper? Was I self-righteous?" [12]

There is also Mrs. Dimble, this large, warm, soft mother—although she has no children of her own—whom Jane has already encountered. We see the motions of charity in her as she and Jane speak of the Dimbles having been forced out of their lovely old house with the advance of the N.I.C.E. upon Edgestow.

> *I'm not a martyr. I'm only an angry old woman with sore feet and a splitting head (but that's beginning to be better) who's trying to talk herself into a good temper. After all, Cecil and I haven't lost our livelihood as poor Ivy Maggs has. It doesn't matter leaving the old house. . . . I shall be better away from it.* [13]

But these attitudes do not come easily. On another occasion where irritation threatens her, Lewis remarks that "if anyone had been watching her expression, they would have seen the little grimace rapidly smoothed out again. Her will had many years of practice behind it" [14]—training and self-training in plain virtues like patience and courtesy. In the odd "transfiguration" scene when Venus descends upon

[11] Ibid., p. 219.
[12] Ibid., p. 224.
[13] Ibid., p. 76.
[14] Ibid., p. 260.

St. Anne's, we see Mother Dimble in garb that reveals what she is. It is like an epiphany: what passes us unobstrusively every day is here unveiled, blazing forth in its true colors. She appears in a robe of a "tyrannous flame color", with a copper brooch and a many-cornered cap.

> For now this provincial wife of a rather obscure scholar, this respectable and barren woman with grey hair and double chin, stood before [Jane] not to be mistaken, as a kind of priestess or sybil, the servant of some prehistoric goddess of fertility—an old tribal matriarch, mother of mothers, grave, formidable, and august.[15]

The point is, she *is* all this. Her fertility has not shown itself in having borne children of her own: rather her office has been to be mother to multitudinous undergraduates, and to Jane, and to be the mother of Charity to whomever she encounters. And this flaming, coppery attire corresponds exactly to the attire on the goddess in the vision which Jane has had, which was a vision of mere disordered appetite and unrestrained sexuality. In the figure of Mother Dimble we find the good thing of which all lust and lechery is a travesty.

There are the Dennistons at St. Anne's as well—probably as close as any to the sort of people Jane might choose for her companions. They are intelligent and civilized, and in them Jane finds quite natural companionship. But she discovers a disarming sort of simplicity in them too. It turns out that, far from being bothered by fog on the day when they had planned to take Jane on a picnic, they both like Weather—"Not this or that kind of weather but just Weather.

---

[15] Ibid., p. 363.

It's a useful taste if one lives in England." They must eat the picnic inside the car, but it is in a scene that spells goodness in any Lewis narrative. "Presently, they left the unfenced road ... and went bumping across grass and among trees and finally came to rest in a sort of little grassy bay with a fir thicket on one side and a group of beeches on the other. There were wet cobwebs and a rich autumnal smell all round them. Then all three sat together in the back of the car and there was some unstrapping of baskets, and then sandwiches and a little flask of sherry and finally hot coffee and cigarettes. Jane was beginning to enjoy herself." [16]

The mediators of these first hints of joy in Jane—in the vexed, harried, grieved Jane—are such things as cobwebs and cigarettes and hot coffee. There is no foolishly simplistic notion here that all will be well if only we can just get a nice cup o' tea: rather, we see the whole drama proceeding in a realm where humble ordinariness is thrown into bright relief against the murky background of the abnormal and the diseased and the sophisticated.

One of the most interesting characters at St. Anne's is Ivy Maggs, the charwoman—although she is not employed at the household in that capacity. She is just a member of the company. In her we find the image of what Lewis transfigured in the scene in *The Great Divorce* where the dreamer sees a great procession of chariots and beasts and music, all honoring a noble and beautiful lady whom he takes to be the Virgin Mary. No: it is only Sarah Smith of Golder's Green, a charwoman. Well then, what is she doing with all that panoply? Oh, that's just the truth about her. All her beauty and virtue were hidden under the common veil of mops and pails before, but that was only temporary. Now

[16] Ibid., p. 113.

you get to see who she really was all along. Her simplicity and integrity and faithfulness—this is what those things really *look like.*

Ivy is like this. Like most of Lewis' plain, good people, she takes traditional morality for granted. She has not been sophisticated out of it. The exchanges between her and Jane are illuminating. At one point she has told Jane about how her husband, before he and Ivy had met, had been guilty of a petty theft. He had "gone straight" ever since, but the theft had been discovered and he was now serving a jail term.

> *Ivy had not seemed conscious of the purely social stigma attaching to petty theft and a term of imprisonment, so that Jane would have had no opportunity to practice, even if she had wished, that almost technical "kindness" which some people reserve for the sorrows of the poor. On the other hand, she was given no chance to be revolutionary or speculative—to suggest that theft was no more criminal than all wealth was criminal. Ivy seemed to take traditional morality for granted.*[17]

This is the sort of thing Jane runs into at St. Anne's, and it throws her enlightened and theoretical liberalism into a watery light.

We also find the sceptic MacPhee in the household at St. Anne's. He has a "shrewd, hard-featured face", and likes to speak in philosophical polysyllables, eternally drawing fine distinctions and insisting on verification of hypotheses. He does not believe in Jane's dreams, or even, it seems, in Ransom's experiences. But his part in the household depends, Ransom tells him, not on his confidence in Ransom but

[17] Ibid., p. 302.

vice versa—on Ransom's confidence in him. And there are
qualities of integrity and loyalty and courage in him that
are clearly "preparation" for grace, so to speak. These are
enough for the moment. Here and elsewhere in Lewis' narratives we come upon this oddity, that a given act or attitude, be it never so inadequate, will do for the moment,
the idea being that this is a step in the right direction and
more will follow in time. It is perhaps analogous to Abraham's groping step in moving out of Ur: he certainly had
very little notion of who Yahweh was, or what he had up
his sleeve. But this small act was "counted unto him for
righteousness", and indeed started the entire snowball of
Faith rolling. The point here is not that MacPhee is an
allegory for Abraham. That would make a jumble out of
the drama here. Rather, what we see about MacPhee seems
to be something that is at work in all possible stories. It is
part of the force of Lewis' narrative technique that the incidents keep suggesting this while at the same time defying
allegorical interpretation.

The figure of Mr. Bultitude the bear, who is also one of
the regulars at St. Anne's, might seem to be pushing things
too far. And it hardly appears that this great snuffly, wheezy
creature encourages very serious comment, or that anything of much dramatic consequence attaches to him. Where
are we? In *A Midsummer Night's Dream* or *Alice in Wonderland*?
Well, perhaps not. But the narrative has moved us into an
order of things in which we find a concord that runs right
across the barriers that ordinarily hem in our daily existence. It will be remarked, in this connection, that Mr. Bultitude is not a *magic* bear. He is not a Narnian Talking Beast:
there is at least the plausibility about his presence that some
animals seem especially open to being trained. (We have all
sorts of stories from Africa of lionesses living amiably with

families.) But that is neither here nor there. Mr. Bultitude's place in the whole pattern of the drama seems to be that he lives on the frontier between the realm, as it were, of England, with Edgestow and Cure Hardy on the one hand, and on the other the ancient, druidical land of Logres and Merlin—that realm where the familiar intercourse between men and nature had not yet been entirely effaced. The household at St. Anne's seems to represent a sort of "earnest" or adumbration of the return to that merry and hospitable order in which courtesies do not stop with our own species.

Lewis devotes too much space in his narrative to the special quality of Mr. Bultitude's experience for us to be able to ignore it. To do so is like ignoring Ariel in *The Tempest*: you may do so, but you are not attending to the drama that Shakespeare happened to write. When MacPhee, for example, speculates, to Ivy's scandal, that the "friendship" between Pinch the cat and Mr. Bultitude may entail even "some obscure transferred sexual impulses", Ransom points out that he is

> introducing into animal life a distinction that doesn't exist there.... You've got to become human before the physical cravings are distinguishable from affections—just as you have to become spiritual before affections are distinguishable from charity. What is going on in the cat and the bear isn't one or other of these two things: it is a single undifferentiated thing in which you can find the germ of what we call friendship and of what we call physical need. But it isn't either at that level.[18]

This touches another theme that runs all through Lewis' narratives and that constitutes a sort of matrix for these narratives. It is that in the plenitude of Nature, from flatworms

[18] Ibid., p. 261.

to seraphim, we see the pattern of Charity arrayed hierarchically, in a diagram as it were. That is, what exhibits itself as mere pulsation or impulse on the lowest levels seems to undergo a refining and separating process as you rise on the scale, so that by the time you get to the higher animals you seem to see something that looks like rudimentary choice, and when you get to humanity you see real freedom, with its corollary choice, and the tension that attends this business of having options. Some dragonfly unites with another dragonfly without the slightest reflection on the matter. But this uniting is a rudimentary case in point of the union that constitutes the very heartbeat of the universe, so to speak, and we humans have all sorts of conscious choices to make in this regard. We may opt, in one area, for either lechery or chastity, a choice that the dragonfly does not have to bother with; or, in another area, we may opt for selfishness (the refusal to "know" other selves) or for hospitality (the greeting of other selves); and so forth. On the highest levels the seraphim seem to live in the presence of the thing which all lower life hints at and human life struggles for (or against), namely pure Charity, which is the state of affairs where fact (the way the City of God is built) and will (the freedom of the creature to assent to that way) are synonymous.

This seems a far cry from Mr. Bultitude lumbering about St. Anne's. But it is not if we grant what is unmistakably at work in the drama here. Here is the sort of language we encounter in a prolonged scene in which Mr. Bultitude experiences "temptation"—or at least as much of temptation as may ever assail an animal.

> *Mr. Bultitude's mind was as furry and as unhuman in shape as his body. He did not remember . . . the provincial zoo. . . .*

He did not know that he loved and trusted [the keepers]
now. He did not know that they were people, nor that he
was a bear. Indeed, he did not know that he existed at all;
everything that is represented by the words I *and* Me *and*
Thou *was absent from his mind. . . . Hence his loves might,*
if you wished, be all described as cupboard loves: food and
warmth, hands that caressed. . . . There was no prose in his
life. . . . One of our race, if plunged back for a moment in
the warm, trembling, iridescent pool of that pre-Adamite con-
sciousness, would have emerged believing that he had grasped
the absolute; for the states below reason and the states above
it have, by their common contrast to the life we know, a
certain superficial resemblance.[19]

It is worth noting the effect on Mr. Bultitude of Ransom and Ivy Maggs respectively. Ransom "had brought back
with him from Venus some shadow of man's lost preroga-
tive to ennoble beasts. In his presence Mr. Bultitude trem-
bled on the very borders of personality", whereas with Ivy,
"he was perfectly at home—as a savage who believes in
some remote High God is more at home with the little
deities of wood and water. It was Ivy who fed him, chased
him out of forbidden places, cuffed him, and talked to him
all day long." [20]

It is easy enough to point out that the vision at work in
this narrative here is the same one which Saint Paul barely
touches on when he gives us those tantalizing hints about
the whole creation groaning under some sort of bondage,
waiting for some sort of freedom of which our deliverance
seems to be the firstfruits. On this accounting, it is human

[19] Ibid., p. 306.
[20] Ibid., pp. 307, 308.

life that stands at the center of the whole drama. Below us there is instinctual disharmony: nature red in tooth and claw; above us there is the warfare among the principalities and powers. But somehow the locus of the business as far as we are concerned is human flesh, and this seems to be for two reasons: first, we, unlike any other creature, share both the animality of the creation below us and the rationality of the creation above us, and it is via choice that we make ourselves and hence our world either angelic or diabolical; and second, the Incarnation focused the drama forever in this human flesh. It is, somehow, a key, this flesh of ours.

All the elements in *That Hideous Strength*, whether they are the forces of tyrannical technological materialism, or those of druidical religion, or those glimpsed in the descent of the gods on St. Anne's, or those at work in Mark and Jane, or in Belbury—all these elements are funneled to a point in the flesh of Jane, the way things in another Story came to a focus in the body of a young woman. Jane, like Mary, or like Psyche, seems to be the God-bearer. Both Belbury and St. Anne's need her: she must choose to which power she will say, "Be it unto me according to thy word."

Once more we seem to have strayed far afield from Mr. Bultitude in his lumberings. But perhaps this gives us a clue to the nature of the drama at work in the narrative. We find ourselves here in a world of images—not allegories, nor paper dolls, nor stereotypes, but images. Everything bespeaks something beyond itself. A bear lumbers about, not carrying a placard announcing "Natural Life", but simply going about his business as a domestic bear might, with this difference, that he happens to exist in a drama which insists on seeing "his business" and indeed his very "bearness" in the light of all the hints ever dropped in our way by myth, history, and revelation. The narrative seems to press upon us the question "How do you wish to see a bear's life?" or perhaps "How might a bear's experience underscore our own?"

The figure of Mr. Bultitude introduces us to a theme that is most vividly to be seen in the matter of Merlin. It is the theme of "no going back". Various other themes feed into it, such as the idea of things thickening and hardening and coming to a point; and the idea of Aslan's refusal ever to tell *what might have been*; and the warning in Narnia against trusting a beast who was once a man; and Ransom not eating the fruit twice in Perelandra, nor listening to a symphony again; and so forth. It all derives from the notion that there is a Story going on, and that to retrace your steps or thumb back through the pages is to refuse somehow the movement of the Story, or worse, the wisdom of the author. The author has a denouement in mind and you must move through the action *at his pace*. Otherwise you will find yourself striving against the author himself, and to be in that position is to refuse both him and the thing he has made. It is what Lucifer did.

Merlin emerges from the ancient and harmonious time when the distinction between white and black magic had not yet been introduced. Mankind was still close enough to nature to be "familiar" with it, in all the senses of that word. But that time has gone, along with our innocence; the fabric has been ripped; Eden is lost; and there is no going back. Everything is tainted now, and we must live obedient to the limitations and taboos appropriate to our exile. (For this reason, surely, nudist camps are misconceived: you can't recapture innocence simply by reenacting the external conditions of innocence.) There are regions we cannot tamper with now. Lewis points out that Edgestow lies in the very heart of what had been Logres, and that in fact Merlin's body had been buried in Bragdon Wood. This, it turns out, is why the N.I.C.E. is so keen to secure the property: it has learned about this. The designs of the Institute, far from being merely political or scientific, are diabolical, and its members wish most earnestly to enlist the power that Merlin represents in bringing their grand design to pass. Merlin, coming from that innocent time, is "neutral", or at least he may be thought to be unfamiliar with the stark distinctions between good and evil as they manifest themselves now. So it is of the essence that Belbury get there first in the race to secure Merlin's services.

Jane has seen enough in her dreams for the company at St. Anne's to know what is happening, and so the race is on. Belbury, which has only power in mind, will use any measures that will assist it, legitimate or not. St. Anne's, obedient to the pattern of things, and aware that we may not now "go back" to antiquity with all of its druidical possibilities, must know whether there is a warrant for Merlin to be enlisted, even in the service of the good. As it turns out there is. Merlin asks, "Has not our Fair Lord made it a law for Himself that He will not send down the Powers to mend or mar in this Earth until the end of all things?" . . .

Ransom explains, "But if men by enginry and natural philosophy learn to fly into the Heavens, and come, in the flesh, among the heavenly powers and trouble them, He has not forbidden the Powers to react."[21]

Belbury has removed the protection of that law. It has "broken by natural philosophy the barrier which God of His own power would not break". It is a modern drama here:

---

[21] Ibid., p. 290.

perhaps not since Prometheus has there been quite the spectacle of a grab being made for secrets which the gods reserve to themselves—not until the modern scientific era. Nothing will now be sacrosanct. Nothing will be taboo. Nothing inviolable.

Merlin, having been a magician, a Christian, and hence a penitent (he lived in Britain when Christianity arrived), is the one through whom this once-only passage of power must occur. He has not been dead, however: he has been held in reserve, suspended outside of time, for this hour. But there can be no question of a mere going back to spells and conjurings, and Ransom sharply rejects the suggestion of Merlin that they invoke these—a suggestion that lulls Ransom momentarily with a Lilithlike anesthesia as Merlin coaxes: "Through me ... you can suck up from the Earth oblivion of all pains." [22] Ransom's refusal is based on the following: "Whatever of spirit may still linger in the earth has withdrawn fifteen hundred years further away from us since your time.... In this age it is utterly unlawful."

The disregard for taboo under the rubric of "objectivity", and the metamorphosis of natural philosophy (read "science") into the lust for power (read "*hubris*")—these are the marks of Belbury. But we do not meet them in their obviously grotesque forms at first. We meet them first in Mark.

At our first glimpse of Mark we find him walking toward Bracton. "He did not notice at all the morning beauty of the little street that led him from the sandy hillside suburb where he and Jane lived...." [23] The morning beauty of a little street is precisely what would not impress Mark, trained

[22] Ibid., p. 288.
[23] Ibid., p. 16.

as he is to see concrete things only as data to be assumed into analytic generalizations and abstractions, and preoccupied as he is with the frantic business of winning his way into the Inner Ring at Bracton. He encounters his colleague Curry on the way, and it becomes clear at once that not one syllable of candid, genuine conversation is possible, since Mark must tailor every phrase, indeed every inflection of his voice, to the business of toadying to Curry, for Curry is part of the Progressive Element at Bracton, and Mark will give anything in heaven and earth to be accepted in that circle. This becomes increasingly and painfully clear in every one of Mark's relationships: Feverstone, Straik, Cosser, Fairy Hardcastle—it is all the same. The grisly irony that emerges at once is that, far from being a reward worth winning, this acceptance into the inner ring for which Mark is squandering every pennyworth of his attention, energy, decency, and self-esteem, is a colossal bore. Vacuity. Fatuity. Ennui. The people for whose favor he is prepared to sell his soul turn out to be ciphers and cads. And the course Mark must steer is infinitely tricky: on the one hand he must not, by the faintest hint, suggest that he has any viewpoint differing in the smallest jot from the official viewpoint of the Progressive Element; but on the other, in order to be really *in* he must register ever so artfully and unobtrusively a certain independence, so that he will be considered to be a valuable addition to the circle and not just a lackey. He never seems able to quite hit upon the correct course, and his dismay and forlornness deepen the further in he gets.

We may see something of the quality of the fellowship in this circle in a scene in Curry's rooms with a number of the fellows. The talk has turned upon just what the N.I.C.E. is, and it has become more than clear that only the vaguest notions on this point are possible—something to do with taking "applied science seriously from the national point of view" [24] and of putting "science itself on a scientific basis. There are to be forty interlocking committees sitting every day", and so on and so on, into an egregiously tedious brave new world, complete with a Pragmatometer that will distill and print out all the findings of these committees.

When Mark and Feverstone (*Lord* Feverstone, the Devine we met in *Out of the Silent Planet*) are left alone, Feverstone begins to chuckle, then to laugh, then to roar. Mark can only join him, and oddly, for this once, Mark's reaction is the genuine, spontaneous article: the entire preceding conversation *has* been laughable, and if there is a rag of good sense and humanity left in Mark he will shrug the entire imbecilic business off with a laugh and never give it another moment's attention. The momentary chance at authenticity flicks past, however, as do all other such moments in Mark's descent into hell at Belbury, and Feverstone's reasons for mirth predominate: " 'Pragmatometer—palatial lavatories—practical idealism,' gasped Feverstone. It was a moment of extraordinary liberation for Mark. All sorts of things about Curry and Busby which he had not previously noticed, or else, noticing, had slurred over in his reverence for the Progressive Element, came back to his mind." [25]

And then we are given a glimpse into the quality of the bond at work in this circle: " 'It really is rather devastating' said Feverstone ... 'that the people one has to use for getting things done should talk such drivel ...' " [26] Well: obviously Mark must shift his loyalty, ever so subtly, over to Feverstone. Curry is clearly not in the innermost ring. But

[24] Ibid., p. 37.
[25] Ibid., p. 39.
[26] Ibid.

there is more. When Mark suggests that Curry and company *are* the brains of Bracton nonetheless, Feverstone snorts, "Good Lord no! Glossop and Bill the Blizzard, and even old Jewel, have ten times their intelligence."[27] As it happens, the three fellows of the college named here constitute the traditionalist, obscurantist, reactionary element (in the view of the Progressive Element) that obstructs the forward surge of progress at every point. But Feverstone has not altogether lost the capacity to see intelligence and integrity. He will crush them, of course: but he cannot pretend that his own colleagues in the Inner Ring have anything like the brains or integrity that they have.

It is interesting to note that Mark's very conversation turns into the flattest cant in this milieu. At one point he descends to this inanity: "Oh, I haven't any doubt which is *my* side. . . . Hang it all—the preservation of the human race—it's a pretty rock-bottom obligation."[28] It is more than embarrassing: *Mark* talking of *any* rock-bottom obligation at all, let alone a windy platitude such as that.

The company in the N.I.C.E. is a veritable devil's roster. In the peculiar pageantlike nature of this narrative, each one exhibits some variation on the theme of evil. There is Straik, for example, the visionary, secularizing, radical priest, the very archetype of twentieth-century religious radicalism, who speaks and thinks in fierce slogans that rush over all that is human, the way Attila the Hun rushed across the face of Asia. Mark notes his "dark, lean, tragic face, gashed and ill-shaved and seamed, and the bitter sincerity of his manner".[29] "Do not imagine . . . that I indulge in any dreams of carrying out our programme without violence. . . . We

[27] Ibid.
[28] Ibid., p. 41.
[29] Ibid., p. 78.

are not to be deterred." [30] When Mark ventures to suppose
that the Rev. Mr. Straik naturally looks for the fulfillment
of these dreams in the next world, we have this:

> *With every thought and vibration of my heart, with every*
> *drop of my blood ... I repudiate that damnable doctrine.*
> *That is precisely the subterfuge by which the World ... has*
> *sidetracked and emasculated the teaching of Jesus, and turned*
> *into priestcraft and mysticism the plain demand of the Lord*
> *for righteousness and judgment here and now. ... In that*
> *name [of Jesus] I dissociate myself completely from all the*
> *organized religion that has yet been seen in the world.* [31]

For Straik, the doctrine of resurrection refers to the coming order which the N.I.C.E. is bringing in, and "the Son
of Man" refers to "Man himself, full grown [who] has power
to judge the world—to distribute life without end, and punishment without end." [32]

And there is Wither, the Deputy Director of the N.I.C.E.
He seems harmless enough when we first meet him, but
Mark notes in his large face and watery eyes "something
rather vague and chaotic". We soon find that this is a bell-
wether: Wither's very syntax is a vast and indeterminate mire
quite devoid of meaning. After not more than a minute of
conversation with this man, Mark sees "all the well-knit
schemes and promises of Feverstone ... dissolving into some
sort of mist." With his sagging mouth and dreamy courtesy
and vague eyes and interminable circumlocution, Wither
before long appears for what he is, namely a wraith, a specter, a residue—the detritus left after the solid thing we call

[30] Ibid.
[31] Ibid.
[32] Ibid., p. 128.

a human being has been leeched away by the refusal of truth. We find Wither pacing and humming, here, there, everywhere. He never sleeps. When we see him and Frost locked in an infantile and obscene, even a bestial, embrace, scrabbling and slobbering at each other, we see in a horrible epiphany the inanity and grotesquery that lies at the far end of all the elegant and courtly mendacity that is Wither.

What we see in Wither is the counterfeit of the real detachment of spirit that the mystics speak about. For them this state stands at the far end of the process described by Saint Paul as the crucifixion of the flesh, that is, of the tyranny of mere appetite and impulse. For Wither it means the denial of the validity of the body, and indeed a handing over of all contact with other selves to a sort of automatic mechanism of external courtesies. It is, in other words, the denial of Charity. His spirit now floats in the solitary limbo that lies at the far end of this withdrawal from real, concrete contact with other selves.

Fairy Hardcastle, the head of the secret police at the N.I.C.E., is the very archetype of the perversion of nature at work in Belbury. She is, to be sure, a woman, but everything about her contradicts any image of femininity that has ever existed in human imagination: her "stoker's or carter's hand grip", her short-skirted military uniform, her iron-gray short-cropped hair, her square face and deep voice and cigar—it all stands over against the images of femininity that we have seen in Mother Dimble, Camilla Denniston, and indeed in Jane herself. From Belbury's point of view, of course, there is nothing notable here. What could be more natural? But from the point of view of St. Anne's, there is something awry in this parody of masculinity. The real strength of womanhood (St. Anne's might point out) does not need to *masquerade* this way, nor to ape some tough images of maleness. After all, neither Antigone nor the Virgin Mary needed hobnailed boots or cigars to make their point.

In Fairy Hardcastle we see one more variation on the theme of the unnatural which seems to prevail at Belbury. Here the ancient idea of womanhood seems to have been ripped away from the look of the thing. Why (some seer might inquire) *do* women not have the hard muscles and hairy skin of men? Does it mean weakness—or might it mean that the particular forms in which womanhood bears and exercises strength are quite other than the forms that need bulging muscles? What has gone awry when we find womanhood *aping* this masculine image? What is there about the image that attracts the emulation of a woman like Fairy Hardcastle?

The physiologist Filostrato also presents a variation on this theme of the unnatural, or of that repugnance toward nature. It is apt and ironic that he should be a physiologist, but his entire goal in life is to fumigate the earth. Just as the priest Straik in his apostasy represents the complete reversal of his own vocation, so the physiologist Filostrato is the one who wants to sterilize the world from all these weeds and trees and leaves and eggs—all this fecundity. The point for him is that organic life has served its function of producing Mind, and now it must be jettisoned. "We do not want the world any longer furred over with organic life ... all sprouting and budding and breeding and decaying." [33] We must learn, he says, "to make our brains live with less and less body". Once more we see the gnostic theme of disgust with nature and the flesh, which animates Belbury, and which stands so starkly over against the dumpy and

[33] Ibid., p. 173.

merry affirmation of the flesh at St. Anne's. The irony here, of course, is that all this pale and vitiated cerebralism at Belbury drives straight toward such phenomena as torture, vivisection, the unnatural preservation of the Head, and the final apocalypse when the whole thing explodes in blood and entrails. It is as though there were some judgment devised by some great dramatist, in which the punishment not only fits the crime but is simply the crime itself turned back on the perpetrator. If you will reject and violate Nature— Nature in all of its manifestations, from plain trust between two people to kindness to animals to true sexuality and even to anatomy itself—then Nature will spring back upon you and destroy you, which is what happens with the unleashing of the animals at Belbury.

In Belbury we have the very map of evil. Belbury with its arcana and secrets; Belbury with its "thoughtful people" and scrapping of all traditions and stifling of all deep-set repugnances; Belbury with its boldness and objectivity; Belbury with its vivisection and torture, all papered over with euphemism and cant about "remedial treatment"; Belbury with its "impulse to reverse all reluctances and to draw every circle anti-clockwise" [34] (contrast this with Ivy Maggs' provincial prudery that is still capable of being scandalized); Belbury with its ill-proportioned room where not one angle is true and not one circle is regular—so that you will get *accustomed* to the nonnatural; Belbury with its spitting on crucifixes and its tearing down of forests and its rechanneling of rivers, and Wither's ghastly talk of the happy family there; and finally Belbury, enshrining the apotheosis of this gnostic *hubris*, the slobbering Head: Mind! Freed from Body! Man on the throne, jetti-

[34] Ibid., p. 269.

soning the Creation, becoming like the gods—pure spirit—
God himself!

It is a tedious and very old story, on whose theme all
tragedy and all sin constitute mere variations.

Over against this hatred for Creation and its goodness
stands the most dazzling scene in the narrative. It is the
descent of the gods on St. Anne's. It has already become
clear that we humans are not the highest powers there are,
and that Ransom is not only in touch with *eldils* but that
he is receiving orders from this realm. The struggle with
Belbury, right down to the politics in the Common Room
at Bracton and the race for Merlin, is the local and immediate face of a much bigger struggle that goes on among
principalities and powers. This is exalted and hence difficult terrain for fiction; but the idea that it is inappropriate
matter for narrative is only a recent one in history.

In this scene we find in great colorful chunks, we might
almost say, the themes that animate all of Lewis' imagination and moral vision. The gods are the very epiphany of
the plenitude that lies about us every day all day, in language (from chitchat to the highest poetry), and in color
and smell and shape, and in nuzzling and tickling and making love, and in water and sleep and dancing and logic and
geometry and tears and Charity. Lewis worked at this theme
in his poetry, e.g., in "Le Roi S'amuse", and "Pan's Purge",
and "The Planets", and "On Being Human". All of them
celebrate the sheer *texture* of life. It is all a way of echoing
"*Benedicite! omnia opera Domini!*" In the scene at St. Anne's,
we find two variations on the theme—an "upstairs" and
a "downstairs", with Ransom and Merlin up in the Blue
Room seeing the glories unfurled under titanic modalities
that the little group in the kitchen downstairs would hardly
be able to cope with. Mercury arrives, and the group in

the kitchen find themselves punning and chattering and altogether carried away with the sheer delight of *talk*; upstairs Ransom and Merlin find themselves

> *within the very heart of language, in the white-hot furnace of essential speech. All fact was broken, splashed into cataracts, caught, turned inside out, kneaded, slain, and reborn as meaning. For the lord of meaning himself, the herald, the messenger, the slayer of Argus, was with them: the angel that spins nearest the sun. Viritrilbia, whom men call Mercury and Thoth.*[35]

The epiphany goes on, upstairs and downstairs, page after page, with the descent of Venus (Charity) and Mars (Valor) and Saturn (sheer time and antiquity) and Jove ("kingship and power and festal pomp and courtesy shot from him as sparks fly from an anvil"[36]). The mortals at St. Anne's find themselves "caught up into the *Gloria* which those five excellent Natures perpetually sing".[37]

This—over against what we see at Belbury. Joy over against horror. Paradise over against hell.

But the point of it all for Lewis' narrative is to be found in the marriage relationship of Mark and Jane. Put it this way: left to himself—his cloddish disregard for Jane, his egoism, his pusillanimity, his ignominious crawl toward the vacuous Inner Ring, his secularism—left to this, Mark will land in Belbury forever, for that is the only place where such a frame of mind can be at home, the ironic damnation being that this "home" is the hideous antithesis of all possible homes, the Miserific Vision itself. And on the other

[35] Ibid., p. 322.
[36] Ibid., p. 327.
[37] Ibid.

hand Jane, vexed and confused and irritated and nettled by life generally—Jane is dragged into the last thing she wants, namely Charity. Salvation. (It is also ironic, of course, that Mark will give almost anything to win his way into Belbury, while Jane will give almost anything to stay out of St. Anne's. Both must experience the reversal of their designs.)

We may observe the movement of the drama—the movement of Mark and Jane back toward each other—by noting the steps each is obliged to take. Jane, who begins with the natural wish for self-determination, and very little notion that her womanhood, her flesh, has much to do with anything, finds herself sent to school, so to speak, at St. Anne's. Her capacity to "see", manifest in her dreams, embroils her in the struggle against Belbury which is, in effect, a struggle against Mark and all that entraps him. By being the agent of his destruction, she becomes the agent of his salvation.

And Mark, having all but sold his soul, salvaged and delivered from the toils of Belbury, moves back toward the Jane to whom he had been pledged in the sacrament of matrimony, that great school of Charity, but which sacrament has so far for him been a hollow form devoid of the solid meaning of which it is meant to be the vehicle. Again and again it is the mere memory of Jane which plucks Mark by the sleeve, or reminds him of the reality of which Belbury is the ghastly travesty.

It is not for nothing that the last scene in the narrative fulfills what the first scene lacks—that wretched first scene with Jane, solitary and frustrated, musing on the words from the Prayer Book about matrimony. Now the two are delivered to each other in a scene of unabashed eroticism—baptized eroticism, we might say. Jane goes to Mark, into the very landscape of Venus,

... *into the liquid light and supernatural warmth of the garden and across the wet lawn (birds were everywhere) and past the see-saw and the greenhouse and the piggeries, going down all the time, down to the lodge, descending the ladder of humility . . . to meet and love the penitent Mark who has arrived here, like a shriven pilgrim, thinking quite correctly, "Surely I must have died."* [38]

[38] Ibid., p. 382.

CHAPTER SIX

Till We Have Faces:
The Uttermost Farthing

In a small prefatory paragraph to the 1956 Geoffrey Bles edition of *Till We Have Faces*, Lewis speaks of his tale as a "reinterpretation of an old story". It is just that: Lewis has taken the old story of Cupid and Psyche and, keeping the ancient world as its locale, has given it probably as rich and complex a rendering as the story has ever had, or that it could conceivably support.

Lewis stands here in a poetic tradition that needs no defense. It is an ancient and universal practice for a poet ("poet" here in the Greek sense of "maker", that is, any writer of imaginative things, whether those things find their form in what we would technically call poetry, or in prose) to lift his story bodily from some other poet, or from a whole lineage of poets. Chaucer borrowed a great many of his plots from his forerunners, Shakespeare took almost all of his from prior sources, and of course Ovid's whole work was a matter of retelling stories that were in the air, so to speak. There is really no such thing as making up a wholly new story in any event: we are told that there are only ten or a dozen possible plots in the whole world. Every narrative presents some variation on those few, basic patterns.

The old story that Lewis here reinterprets for us is the story of Cupid and Psyche, and he was not the first to pick up this tale. The only telling of the story itself which we have from antiquity is that of Apuleius, the Latin poet of the second century A.D., in his *Metamorphoses*, or *The Golden Ass*, which is a romance in eleven books. Lewis has kept quite close to the story as Apuleius tells it. Of course the figures of Cupid and Psyche had been around for many centuries before that. Cupid is a Latin poetical version of the figure of Eros, who had appeared as far back as Hesiod and Homer, in the eighth and seventh centuries B.C. in Greece. Hesiod, in his *Theogony*, collects and tells the stories of the beginnings of gods, the universe, and men, and makes Eros one of the oldest of the deities, along with Earth (Ge), the Underworld (Tartarus) and perhaps even Chaos himself. Eros was certainly one of the most powerful deities in this early accounting. Somewhere in there he became, for obvious reasons, connected with Aphrodite, the goddess of love and beauty, better known to us nowadays as Venus. But the picture of Eros as Cupid, the fat baby with the bow and arrows, comes very late. He is originally a remote, perilous, and sublime deity, to be dreaded, not dandled. It is an intriguing business in fact: Eros grows younger with the passage of centuries, that is, younger in the way the poets imagine him. He begins in the archaic period as an almost ineffable deity, then appears in the classical period as a sublimely beautiful youth, then finally as the Hellenistic "putto", or infant boy. Very early on, the poetess Sappho speaks of Eros as "bittersweet", a most telling observation. Plato in the *Symposium* and *Phaedrus* records prolonged discussions among the characters as to just what sort of a thing Eros is. In these discussions we find Eros and Psyche (the soul) being connected. There were cults of Eros at Athens, Thebes, and Thespiae, often in his role as the patron of love between men. Psyche for her part shows up fairly early in the Greek idea of the soul (that is what the word *psyche* means). The soul seems always to be conceived of as female, which of course may arouse speculation in us about this image of the soul as suggesting fairly accurately the whole capacity of us mortals to see and receive the approaches of the god, who, being male, initiates the approaches, in a way not unlike the picture of Ge, the Earth (female), receiving the approaches of Uranus, the Heavens (male)—although in some versions she also spawns this spouse and thus becomes a sort of Mother of God—or the picture in the Christian vision of the woman receiving the approaches of the deity at the Annunciation and, in a mystery, herself then becoming the *theotokos*, the Mother of God. Spouse and offspring seem somehow to converge. That which is begotten turns out to have been the begetter. One way or another, the ancient tales and rites seem to have caught the idea which at first seems entirely confusing but which turns out to be entirely familiar to anyone who has ever loved, namely that love begets love, or that by loving we learn to love; that love is born in us by our having been loved; and that the fruit of love is love.

It is interesting that a story so rich in its suggestiveness does not appear in Ovid, the one among the ancient writers who brought all these stories together in the form best known to the rest of history, namely his *Metamorphoses*. Only Apuleius tells it. He tells the story of the princess, youngest of three sisters, who was so beautiful that the people worshipped her, thus rousing the jealousy of Venus, who brought about Psyche's exile to the mountain, where she is to be delivered over to some indescribable renegade lover. The one assigned to bring all this about is Venus' son Cupid, who, however, himself falls in love with Psyche and takes her as his bride on the mountain, giving her a palace and visiting her only in the dark of night so that she never sees his face. Her sisters, whom Psyche has wanted to see, eventually visit her and persuade her to disobey her lover and have a peek at him. She does so, with an oil lamp, but, shaken by his supernal beauty, she spills a drop of hot oil on the shoulder of the sleeping god. He awakens and forsakes her, and she goes into desolate exile. Venus pursues Psyche, forcing her to undertake a series of impossible tasks: sorting great heaps of seeds; gathering wool from man-eating sheep; obtaining a jar of water from the Styx; and finally, getting from Proserpine, the goddess of the Underworld, a box of Proserpine's beauty. Psyche is helped, one way and another, in all of these perils, and the final outcome is that she is made immortal and united by the kindness of Jove with Cupid, her lover.

The surprising thing about the story is that it does, finally, end up happily. One has lost hope a thousand times along the way. We may suppose, if we wish, that here there is perhaps a fleeting acknowledgment that joy and not desolation is the very last word. There are other poetical witnesses to this notion, the most dazzling being of course Dante. It is an idea that encompasses tragedy, and drives beyond it.

Lewis has taken this old tale, and has, he says, given it a reinterpretation. This is quite true, for no other writer has done with it quite what Lewis has, although both Walter Pater and William Morris picked up the tale in the nineteenth century and retold it. Lewis says that the story had lived in his mind for many years, "thickening and hardening". That is very much the process, in Lewis' imagination, by which something inchoate and embryonic and vague comes to its fruition and maturity. Attitudes, for example, do this: Eustace, querulous, pusillanimous, and selfish in his habitual little-boy attitudes, thickens and hardens into a dragon, which is what he really is, in any case; Edmund, cruel and obnoxious and perfidious in tiresome little-boy ways, thickens and hardens into a traitor like Judas Iscariot; Mark Studdock, trained to detach data from morals and sentiment, only just escapes becoming a damned soul; Wither, for years skirting and evading the solid truth by circumlocution and tergiversation, thickens and hardens with supreme and ghastly irony into a wraith, so that we see what formerly existed as hardly perceptible little habits of mind and syntax becoming hideously visible as a specter; Weston, megalomaniacally pursuing objectivity and finally power at the cost of truth and charity, thickens and hardens into a monster; general secular utopianism thickens and hardens into Belbury.

In Lewis' vision all evils, no matter how minuscule and respectable, eventually thicken and harden into horrors which no pictures by Hieronymos Bosch can possibly exaggerate; and by the same token, all acts of kindness will eventually become visible for what they are, namely glorious and noble. The image of Narnia or of the City of God is the thick, hard reality hinted at in every helping hand or kind word. The promise given in words to Abraham eventually thickens and hardens into the Incarnate Word.

The thing which has thickened and hardened in Lewis' version of the Cupid and Psyche story is an idea, or rather a set of ideas, about freedom. It might go something like this: the thing that stands between the human soul and its final freedom is not the malice of the gods, nor bad luck, nor handicaps, nor anything else like this. It is quite simply that soul's grim insistence on having freedom on its own terms. Independence. Autonomy. Self-determination. Give it a hundred names, but it comes to the same thing. The irony is that what that soul supposes is the enemy, or at least the set of obstructions between itself and freedom, is the love of the gods. But, alas, the only way of discovering that is to stop fighting and surrender. The one condition of joy is obedience.

Told in various ways, of course, this is the theme of virtually all tales of what went wrong at the beginning of the race; and this fissure between what is and what we think we might prefer lies across all drama, poetry, myth, and fiction, because it lies across our experience.

The method of the modern psychological novel, which is commonly what we think of when we think nowadays of "fiction", is to watch what a character does with his awareness of this fissure and to see how he comes to terms with things. The fissure of course is not now thought of in cosmic or mythic or moral terms—for example, the divine decree that forbids you to watch Diana bathing versus your very keen desire to do just that. Rather, it is commonly seen to lie between some awkward cultural or emotional fact (Stephen Dedalus' Dublin Catholicism has taught him thus and so; or Jane Eyre is in love with Mr. Rochester; or Paul Morel's mother is dominating him) and some equally intractable fact (but your Dublin Catholicism never took into account your creative soul, or Mr. Rochester is already married, or you can't grow up dominated that way). The drama in the modern novel may be found by watching the tug-of-war in a character's consciousness across this apparent fissure, and the resolution occurs when he comes to terms with reality (or fails to do so).

The method of fairy tale and myth is quite different. But we must not suppose that the substance of fairy tale and myth is as different from the substance of the modern novel as the difference in method might suggest. Since all narrative and all art arise from real human experience, it is true to say that *Little Red Riding Hood* and *War and Peace* share at least this much, that what happens in the respective stories has its roots in real experience. "Real experience" for most of us may not take the form of wolves or woodcutters, or of Napoleonic wars for that matter. But we keep on reading these stories generation after generation because, somehow, both of them catch something that seems to be lodged forever in our imaginations—something about conflict and threat and peril and deliverance and resolution and so forth. We cannot change the substance of human experience, and hence we cannot change the substance of art. Methods vary, because sensibilities and cultures vary. There is nothing that we can do about substance, however.

What we find going on in a myth, then, we may assume, has everything in the world to do with real human experience. The myths, for all their paraphernalia of gods and groves and wonders, are perhaps the truest stories ever told. We cannot say that *Sons and Lovers* or *Mrs. Dalloway* are "truer" than the stories of Orpheus or Medea. We can say only that our story tellers nowadays do not find themselves particularly able to make much use of the scenery and methods found in the tales of Orpheus or Medea. They must try to come at our experience in terms that seem to lie close to the look of that experience today.

The obvious difference in method between myth and novel lies right on the surface. The real action in the novel takes place inside (this, of course, refers to "serious" novels: sheer adventure stories have never been granted the dignity enjoyed by the works of Jane Austen, Tolstoy, or Henry James). The action in a myth takes place entirely outside, on the surface.

And this is true on more than one level. That is, by "inside" we do not mean merely inside the protagonist's mind as opposed to what happens in the carriage between London and Bournemouth: we mean that the significance, the importance, of the external event in the novel is altogether in the service of what is going on in the protagonist's consciousness. Henry James is never going to digress into a fish market simply because one lies not far from where Milly Theale lives: if you find yourself in a fish market in a James novel, you may depend upon it that something about the smell and the noise and the generally clammy ambience *answers* to, or *underscores*, or *anticipates* something that is happening in Milly's life.

In a myth, though, when you rush through a grove it is because the chase went in that direction and groves tend to lie across one's path in that landscape. Your Homer or your Ovid is not going to spend much time establishing the atmosphere of the grove: he may tell you that there were cypress and olive trees, and he may note the rocks and a brook and some sheep; but he does not see the grove as a sort of paradigm of the protagonist's situation.

On the other hand, precisely because the entire locale of the myth is "on the surface", there is a wider and deeper sense in which the setting *does* answer to the dramatic situation. Aeneas goes down and down, into darker and more horrifying shadows, on his descent to the Underworld; and Virgil may make the path lie quite unabashedly past whatever beetling crags and under the eaves of whatever forest he likes, not because those features of the landscape *mean* anything, or are symbols, but rather because the whole world, of form and meaning, or of substance and accidents, or of event and significance, is one seamless fabric. Aeneas is going down into those shadows, not because Virgil needs to vivify the notion of mystery and terror: he is going down there because *that is where Hades is*. Hades is not a symbol for Aeneas' dark night of the soul, or for his passage to maturity, or for anything else. It is a real place. The sea, for Ulysses, does not "represent" his great quest in life: it happens to be the geography over which he must sail in order to get home. Our later ideas of terror, or of quest, find thickness and hardness, we might say, in the real geography of myth.

One way of making clear the stark difference in method between myth and the novel, or, more fundamentally, between the mythic (say "ancient") way of seeing everything and the modern way, is to point out the following contrast: to a modern man a glittering alpine peak might suggest the feeling or the state of exaltation, and he might suppose that the peak supplies us with a good metaphor, which it does of course. At the root of myth, however, lies the idea that exaltation is a feeling appropriate to a great eminence like this peak. It is a question of *which precedes which*. The peak is there, and then appropriate feelings about it. Hades is there, and then our terrors. Or put it this way: the exaltation "means" that there are peaks—real peaks— somewhere; terror "means" that there is something terrifying somewhere—say, Hades. The external is prior to the internal and therefore more basic, on the mythic view. External reality is the fixity, the given: we must find out about *it*, and come to terms with it. Our experience, and our feelings, are posterior to, and therefore subordinate to, external reality. The gods demand our obedience: they are not projections of either our needs or our desires. Rather, those needs and desires are hints in us of what things may be like outside. (Anyone who has read Lewis' *The Discarded Image* or *The Abolition of Man* will recognize this whole line of thought here.)

In *Till We Have Faces* we have the story of a woman named Orual, who has a complaint against the gods. Straight off we have a clue to Lewis' method in his telling of this tale. We are hearing it all from the point of view of someone who has been *left out* of the good things happening. We have always heard the story of Cupid and Psyche told with the focus on Psyche and her joys and sorrows. Suddenly we find that we are looking at it all from the point of view of an outsider; or worse yet, not only from an outsider, but from an outsider who will never be allowed in: at least for the moment there is not the smallest hint of any such thing.

One way or another this unhappy sense of having been left out or snubbed by the gods lies at the root of almost every evil in any story. The protohistoric sin of *hubris* which we find in tragedy, or of pride which we find in Lucifer, or of ambition which we find in Macbeth—indeed, the very love of money, which, we are told, lies at this root and which has for its only use the buying of our way into the palace of pleasure—are these not all variations on the theme of Orual's complaint against the gods, which is that they have not been *fair*? There are privileges to which she has not been admitted. There are secrets which she needed to know in order to accomplish what they demanded, but which they, with ineffable cynicism, would not tell her. Life has dealt her a poor hand. Disadvantage, ugliness, or, for the rest of us, poverty, obscurity, handicap—the tricks that the gods have up their sleeves to keep us from joy are innumerable, and if they will not favor us, then there's no one left but ourselves to seize the situation and wrest joy from it.

Orual's complaint is like that. But there is more. We come upon her story at the end, after she has long since adopted the most heroic posture possible it would seem, namely, utter unsentimentalism. She will not pity herself (she says). She will ask nothing. She will hide any residual womanly or human softness inside a carapace of sheer objectivity. She is merely the neutral observer now, charting dispassionately the cruelty and anger of the gods and presenting it as incontrovertible evidence for our cool judgment. *They* are angry with *her*, and with no cause in heaven or earth except that they have chosen her to be angry with. She has nothing at all to lose by daring to accuse the gods now, since there is nothing left with which they can hurt her: no husband, no children, no happiness, no fortune. She is invulnerable. She is blameless. She is asking for no pity. And she is of all creatures the most desolate.

Orual's complaint, really, is that the gods have been unfair. They have been unfair, she says, because they have not told her enough, and one can hardly be expected to know what is going on or how to act with no *clues*. Implicit in this very plausible complaint is a prior one which we are not sure Orual is quite prepared to own, namely that the gods have been unfair in making her ugly, and in picking Psyche for privileges unavailable (she supposes) to Orual. And to make matters worse, "there is no judge between gods and men, and the god of the mountain will not answer me", she insists.

And we may have a further hint here as to the nature of the drama Lewis is setting up. Orual is implacable, and, it would seem, with very good reason. She has all the data on her side. All she has to do is to enumerate it, point after remorseless point, and anyone in heaven and earth will see how cynical the gods are, and how blameless Orual is. She is in a quite unassailable position to make her accusation. She will tell all, and that will constitute an accusation.

The gigantic irony that presides over the entire tale, however, is that this "telling all" which Orual assumes will add up to an accusation against the gods, becomes, without the gods having to alter a syllable or add a single footnote, Orual's own self-condemnation. Somehow (where did the case go wrong? Where?) this log, this catalogue of the gods' machinations constitutes a serene indictment of Orual. She has told the truth too successfully, and the truth damns her.

We do not get very far into the tale before we begin to see that a complex drama is a-building. Without ever moving away from the sort of narrative that we might expect from this princess in a barbarian land, Lewis brings together what looks like a Gordian knot of themes: there is the intrusion of the gods into the citadel of the self; there is Orual's blameworthy missing of all the signs and her charge of "unfair" against the gods; there is the frightening spectacle of love turning into tyranny and thence to hate, the whole process entirely unrecognizable to itself; there is the pellucid wisdom of the Greeks versus the dark and bloody wisdom of barbarian cult; there is the disturbing set of cryptic and oracular utterances, "You also shall be Psyche" or "You are Ungit", etc.; there is the almost imperceptible unfolding of the transfiguring process whereby, lo and behold, it turns out that Orual, for all of her bitterness and hatred, actually bears the burden of Psyche's salvation; and there is the piercing theme of *sehnsucht*—that "sweet desire" for the Gardens of the Hesperides—that flashes like summer lightning through all of Lewis' work.

Something of the manner in which mythic narrative does its work emerges when we note the fact that these "themes", which touch on virtually every aspect of the human dilemma, become apparent without our ever having to move off the surface of the narrative. There are no symbols and no allegories, as far as the narrative itself is concerned. It is we, later, who, because we have chosen to live in a world whose only realities are psychological, must chatter brightly about Ungit "representing" the dark forces of nature, or about the Fox "representing" the wisdom of the Greeks, and so forth. At least part of the force of narrative like this is that, without ever saying a syllable on the topic, it calls into question the sort of *world* the reader is assuming.

The narrative does this in a twofold way. First it calls our (modern) world into question by simply ignoring our world as even a possibility. By no smallest demurral, by no hint that it may not all be exactly, literally, as it seems to be in Glome, and by no apology on the author's part, no knowing glance or wink thrown in our direction—by all of this the story proceeds on its implacable mythic way, and it is we who must paw Reality by the sleeve and say, "But of course you're not like that at all, are you? Or if you seem to be like that, it's only a matter of symbol, isn't it? It's all lies of poets, isn't it?"

And suddenly we find ourselves impaled with the second prong of the fork: for no sooner are the words off our lips than we realize we have lifted the objection, *ipsissima verba*, from the lips of the Fox, the rationalist who, though he was very wise, was unable to see most of the reality that swirled so dangerously about them all. The story not only never recognizes the possibility that a world like ours (and the Fox's) really exists: it includes in itself the touching portrait of a character who supposes that such a world does exist and that it is the real world. Or put it this way: the notion—the Fox's notion, our notion—that old tales of the gods are only symbolic, albeit very fruitfully and profoundly symbolic, is itself thrown into a pathetic light.

Orual's quarrel with the gods focuses on the goddess Ungit and her son, the Brute. But we cannot put it that way without immediately starting to qualify things. For it is very far from clear just who or what Ungit is, or how we are to think of her. She is, so to speak, a black stone, like a great slug, who sits in a dark and smoky temple across the river Shennit from Glome, the city in which Orual's father, the churlish Trom, is king. But then no one quite knows whether Ungit *is* that stone, or whether that stone merely localizes her presence. She, or it, is without head or hands or face, and she is "a very great goddess". We find that the Greek slave, the Fox, who is tutor to Trom's three daughters, believes that Ungit is the same deity whom his countrymen call Aphrodite. To him and to us, of course, this clears things up: ah—the goddess of love and beauty. Our familiar friend Venus.

But if Ungit is Venus, she is a much darker, more bloody, more earthy deity than the lithe and statuesque figure we know from the Greeks and Romans. Indeed, the Fox himself suggests that she is more like the Babylonian than the Greek Aphrodite, since Ungit's cult is a smelly and messy affair, all reeking of burned hair and fat, stale incense, wine, and blood. The Greeks, at least the later, more rationalistic Greeks, tended to fumigate the pantheon. The more rhetorical and sophisticated they got, the less terror they felt, and the more light suffused the pantheon. This, of course, would seem to be reasonable—one of the marks we would hope to see attending the progress of man from savagery to civilization. The more reasonable we become, the less we are inclined to strangle chickens and goats and to sprinkle their blood about on stocks and stones. The more we stand tall as primates, the less we are inclined to grovel. The more we learn of natural processes, the less whimsical and terrible things seem.

The Fox is a harbinger of this sort of thing in Glome. He knows the old tales, but they are "poetry" to him, that is to say, lies. He tells Orual the Greek story of how

Aphrodite loved the prince Anchises, and how she lay with him and how he was terror-stricken upon finding that it had been a goddess with whom he had lain, begging her to kill him. (*We* know that the child conceived then was Aeneas: all Anchises knew was the terrifying fact that no mortal can enjoy this sort of intimacy with the gods and survive. Of course, he was quite wrong, and his terror quite misbegotten.) The Fox, whom Orual can clearly see has lost himself altogether in the narrative, deepening and lilting his voice as he tells it, comes to himself at the end and demurs: "Not that this ever really happened.... It's only lies of poets, lies of poets, child. Not in accordance with nature."[1] But Orual can also see that this story has touched something in the Fox that lies deeper than his stoic reasonableness, and that, if the goddess whom the Greeks call Aphrodite appears more beautiful in Greece than in Glome, "she was equally terrible in each".

In the Fox's view, nature turns out to be thought of as a hospitable and harmonious scheme, according to which things will arrange themselves manageably and predictably, if not always entirely comfortably for us. It is at least a tidy and a clean scheme. And if we will but observe how nature proceeds, we will see that there is a gratifying correspondence between that procedure and our minds. Things are *reasonable*. Harvest follows seedtime, not because we have sufficiently placated the capricious gods, but because that is how things work. Heavens, child! You don't suppose there is any *serious* connection between sacrifice and harvest?

Thus the Fox's teaching. But again and again, by a faraway look or even a tear in his eye, and certainly by this lilt

[1] C. S. Lewis, *Till We Have Faces* (Grand Rapids, Michigan: William B. Eerdmans Publishing Co., 1964), p. 8.

in his voice when he gets to singing songs about apple-laden lands—time and again he betrays his case. His teaching is excellent stuff for developing courage and equanimity and fortitude and patience, and it contains great and salutary wisdom. But it does not reach all the way down. Those old songs now—those lies of the poets: their very falsity bespeaks heights and depths and glories and terrors in the light of which the Fox's reasonable maxims look meager and pale.

On the other hand we find the old priest of Ungit. There he is, ridiculously decked in bladders and feathers and amulets and masks, mumbling incantations and insisting on blood, and generally moving through the story cloaked in mystery and fear. Not that *he* is afraid, mind you: he has spent too much time inside the shrine, with the blood and smoke of the cult of Ungit, to feel fear the way we outsiders might. For him, fear means something like what it meant to a tribe not too far from Glome, namely the Hebrews, who when they spoke of "the fear of the Lord" had in mind the settled awareness that the god is a very great god who knows exactly what he (she, in Glome's case) is doing, and who might extinguish you in the process, but who can be trusted to know what he is about. It is not the craven wincing of the schoolboy caught smoking and hauled into the headmaster's study: it is the attentive and expectant obedience of the servant who knows that his master can, and very well may, do anything, and that whether that "anything" appears reasonable or calamitous to the servant, the master is under no obligation to explain or justify what he is doing.

Because the old priest lives in this sort of world, he is not impressed with the blustering vagaries of the poltroon Trom. If you face the abyss day after day, you will not worry about a mere local king and his threats. Rags of the ineffable seem to hang like a ghostly armor about the old priest. He is affected neither by the king's posturings nor the Fox's syllogisms. He simply brings the news to Trom that the blight lies on the land because there is someone Accursed abroad, who must be found, and offered as the Great Offering to the Brute, the shadowy son of Ungit, who lives on the mountain and who has been seen in the land lately, and who demands a spotless victim for the Offering, who will be made his Supper, his Spouse, and so forth and so forth. This is all well-trodden terrain for the old priest, but as he speaks, "the holiness and the horror of divine things were continually thickening in that room." [2]

And the Fox interposes, with enlightened and liberating common sense. This is all the most atrocious nonsense.

> *A shadow is to be an animal which is also a goddess which is also a god, and loving is to be eating—a child of six would talk more sense. And a moment ago the victim of this abominable sacrifice was to be the Accursed, the wickedest person in the whole land, offered as a punishment. And now it is to be the best person in the whole land—the perfect victim—married to the god as a reward. Ask him which he means. It can't be both.* [3]

The disturbing thing is that apparently it can. The priest is not discomfited. All this that the Fox urges is vastly plausible, O King, to be sure: but this wisdom brings no rain or corn. Sacrifice is necessary for that. The trouble with the Greeks is that they suppose they have got things explained, but "holy places are dark places.... Holy wisdom is not clear and thin like water, but thick and dark

---

[2] Ibid., p. 49.
[3] Ibid., pp. 49, 50.

like blood." [4] The wild nature of things may be caught more accurately in the conundrums of the cult of Ungit than in the syllogisms of the Fox.

But we anticipate the story. What of Orual and her sisters? For it is they who are caught up into this drama that gathers over the small kingdom of Glome. Orual is the eldest. She is ugly, and she sees her pretty sister Redival as a hussy. Their mother dies, but presently the king takes a new wife who lives just long enough to bear him yet another daughter, the princess Istra, or as the Greeks would have it, Psyche. The advent of Psyche, Orual tells us, was "the beginning of all my joys".

A promising enough statement. But we have not got two paragraphs into Orual's account of her love for this infant before we hear grating noises. Orual loves Psyche so much that she takes over the case of Psyche from the whole rout of wet nurses and domestics. "I soon had the child out of their hands." [5] And into my own, she might have added.

She cares for Psyche. She wants to be Psyche's mother. She wishes she were a boy so that Psyche could fall in love with her. She takes up Psyche's cause against the harridan Redival every time. For her the very pronoun "we" means herself and Psyche, or the threesome of herself, Psyche, and the Fox. She does not want Psyche to exhibit any trace of maturity, since that will suggest that Psyche is growing older, and perhaps moving out of the category "childhood" where she can be safely kept as Orual's own private possession. Psyche must not love anything or anyone else.

This is all there, right on the surface of the case Orual is putting together against the gods. And it is an entirely famil-

[4] Ibid., p. 50.
[5] Ibid., p. 21.

iar business to anyone who has ever been possessed by desire for someone: what begins as strong and selfless somehow proceeds by some maddening, tragic, and vile metamorphosis, to look more and more consuming, then tyrannous, then frenzied, then cruel, and finally murderous. Love has, somehow, become indistinguishable from hatred.

The thing which Orual cannot cope with is any suggestion that Psyche has any existence at all that she does not owe to Orual. There must be no distance between the two—so that when it turns out that the plague on the people of Glome will yield to the healing hands of Psyche, and they hail Psyche as a goddess, Orual's proper religious concern over whether or not this won't make the gods jealous (they get jealous—something the Fox's wisdom stops short of) begins to spill over into the fear that Psyche is slipping away, and then into plots as to how to keep her.

One other development nettles Orual. When Psyche, from having walked among the plague-ridden people all day, laying hands on them, is struck down with the fever herself, she babbles in her delirium of her gold and amber palace on the mountain. Only fantasies, of course: but what is this desire for something *else*? What is the nature of this fugitive bliss that haunts her?

The spotless Psyche turns out to be the Accursed, of course, since she made herself a goddess and the gods won't have that. From Orual's point of view it is all horrible: Psyche had healed the people, and blessed them, and taken their diseases upon herself, and now this, with the very rabble whom she has healed crying out for her blood. The language draws very close to the other Story of the suffering prince who took the plague of the populace on himself, and was sacrificed to their law because he made himself a

god. The same oddities have a way of cropping up in tale
after tale, especially in ancient tales.

When the sacred lot falls on Psyche, Trom reveals himself for what he is, namely a brute, a fraud, and a coward.
He at first rails, then pretends to be the grief-smitten father
from whom has been asked the unthinkable sacrifice, then
betrays his own relief that the lot has not fallen on him.
Over against this stands Orual's apparently heroic offer of
herself in Psyche's stead. There is no question of this, however: the king leads Orual to a mirror and this is all that is
needed to show her that she cannot hope to be a stand-in
when what the gods have asked for is a perfect specimen.
Her ugly face makes a mockery of any heroic notions she
might have had about being a worthy offering to the god.
And so Orual must stand aside, as it were, and watch, wringing her hands and tearing her hair, while Psyche's story
unfolds: Psyche taken away from Orual; Psyche taken to
the mountain; Psyche left alone, tied to the tree, and then
disappearing and then reappearing—not, lo and behold, rav-
aged and defiled, but radiant and blooming.

None of this, of course, fits at all into Orual's schedule
of things. The gods are vile—that much we know. Hence
it follows, as the dawn the dark, that they hate us and will
destroy us; and that is what they are doing to my beloved
Psyche who is, after all, mine. Mine, mine, mine. I hate it;
I hate them; I hate her.

Thus is Orual, in her more candid moments. But outbursts
like that have at least the integrity of candor about them.
Orual may be wrong in her reading of the situation, but all
is not lost as long as she is prepared to admit that she does,
in fact, hate the whole business. Most of the time, however, that is not the note struck. Most of the time her narrative has the more subtle (and lethal) goal of self-justification

for its end. Orual will chart everything that happens so that we will see how blameless she is.

But something is awry in the whole enterprise. Nothing goes according to schedule. When Orual visits Psyche in the room in the palace where Psyche is locked before she is taken to the mountain, what she has in mind is to comfort Psyche (she thinks). How does it happen, then, that it is Psyche who ends up comforting Orual? How does it come about that it is Orual who wails, "Oh cruel, cruel! Is it nothing to you that you leave me here alone? Psyche, did you ever love me at all?" [6] What ironic alchemy is at work here that transmutes things thus?

It is of course the botched alchemy of egoism which, just as surely as the alchemy of love, can turn everything into its opposite. The gold of charity becomes the lead of self-pity. Or, conversely, the lead of imprisonment and exile turns, in the saint, into the gold of joy.

There is a small piquance here, for in these tortured scenes between Orual and Psyche, Psyche often calls Orual by her nickname "Maia". As it happens, Maia was a Pleiad, the mother of Hermes by Zeus, and her name means "mother" or "nurse", from the root *mag*, signifying growth or increase. But why this name? Surely things are shriveling up in Orual, not gestating. Surely she is destined to be the mother of nothing—neither in her own view, since clearly the gods have passed her by because she is ugly, nor in our (the readers') view, since we can see what she does not, or rather will not, see, namely that she is busy drying up all the springs of fecundity in herself by everything she does. Why Maia, then?

We are given a clue in a small development that appears just at this time. When Trom takes Orual to the mirror, making bitterly clear that she is not a fit offering, much less spouse, for the god, Orual turns away, stung; and it is just here that she mentions for the first time a small pain in her side. Nothing particular. Neither she nor we take much notice of it. But then it crops up and crops up, like a motif, until there is no mistaking it: something is badly wrong inside of Orual. Perhaps there is some disease. Perhaps something is dying in there.

And indeed it is. The thing which she is big with, namely herself, has got to shrivel and die in a sort of purgatorial reverse-gestation, so that she may be the mother of something not herself. In Apuleius' telling of the tale of Cupid and Psyche, the offspring of their union finally is the child Volupta (Pleasure). Well, Orual: you also shall be Psyche. Orual the mother of Pleasure? Joy coming from *her* womb? She who was bitter becoming the mother of joy? Come.

And so we begin to catch glimpses, flicking onto the stage now and again like heralds of coming events, of a drama that Orual cannot hope at this point to conceive of. As things stand now she knows that the gods are vile and cruel. She knows that they take their pleasure by ravaging us. What will be the process—the drama, say—through which Orual must pass before things look differently to her? We begin to see some hints.

For one thing, we note that the weather improves in Glome the very day Orual's sickness begins. As she leaves Psyche she says, "My pains ... came strongly back upon me." [7] Who can miss the language of women's labor here? And this is when the rains come and the crops revive and the plague disappears. But what sort of shift is this? It is Psyche, is it not, who is the Offering for Glome? It is Psyche,

[7] Ibid., p. 77.

surely, whose pains will redeem Glome? Yes. To be sure. The big drama in the story is the mystery of the sickness of the land, and of Psyche as spotless Offering and Spouse for the Brute, whose loving and devouring come to the same thing. Orual is only a bystander. She is only a barren, sick, ugly, and forsaken woman, doomed to the cruel and passive role of outsider. Alas. There is no story for Orual.

But something odd is afoot. It is surely part of Lewis' achievement here that the exquisitely ironic light in which we begin to see that the focus of the whole drama has shifted onto Orual, and that, somehow, these pains in her are being borne, in a mystery, for Psyche and for Glome—that we begin to see this, not by the author plucking our sleeve and whispering secrets to us that Orual has no way of knowing, but rather by her own recitation. Technically speaking we know no more than she does. We are getting all our facts from her. This is her narrative.

And this bit of literary technique hands to us the key to the whole drama. For the entire point of all this is that the gods do not need to say one more syllable than they have said. They have spoken. We do have the word. Orual's complaint is misbegotten from the start. She is *not* the bystander: indeed she is not. She is not to be allowed that bitter luxury—the luxury of nursing grievances, and of carping and railing and whimpering. She must come to joy. She must. The god desires her. She must be his Spouse, but she will be devoured in the process. She also will be Psyche.

Orual's growth toward Charity, in other words, is what we watch in the drama here, and it is a Charity that turns out to be synonymous with joy. Every impulse pulls her in one direction, and her experience (the gods?) nudge and crowd and drag her all willy-nilly in the other. But of course to speak of Charity with respect to a Greek myth seems to involve us in an anachronism, since the notion of Charity in the sense of self-forgetting and self-sacrificing love is a notion that we do not find extolled in any very explicit way in the stories of Greece. We find courage and honor and fortitude and even some kindness and hospitality and compassion at work, to be sure. But this peaceable business of mere selflessness, where revenge and honor do not seem even to be considerations at all, seems to attach itself to stories other than these of Greece—stories you can find in martyrology and hagiology, say.

This of course raises the question as to what Lewis has done with Apuleius' tale. Has he done violence to it? Has he lifted it altogether away from its native landscape? Has he imported notions alien to anything even hinted at in Apuleius?

It would seem to bring us closer to the truth of the matter if we said that Lewis has done an admittedly bold— even perilous—thing here, but that he has done it without betraying or defacing the original materials. Far from betraying or defacing, in fact, he has pursued possibilities that lay in the tale all along. There is honorable precedent for this, in Chaucer's handling of earlier tales, and Shakespeare's, and in the whole lineage of poets who tried their hand at the Arthurian materials. Lewis has taken a tale of love, seen under its special form of passion—in this case the passion of the gods for us mortals—and, remaining obedient to what is suggested in this, and in the whole idea of the god's desire carrying us beyond the borders of our ordinary life, into the mystery of his own dwelling: remaining obedient to this, Lewis has pressed the inquiry as to what richer notions may be descried in all of this. Does this notion of the god's passion for a mortal, and of the god "carrying away" that mortal—does it touch on suggestions never brought to fruition by the Greeks? Certainly the Greeks told tales like this over and over—Ganymede, Hyacinth, Leda, Daphne, Syrinx—the roster is very long. But what does it *do* to a mortal to find himself loved by the god? The myths will tell us that we may find ourselves feasting on dainties, or employed as a cupbearer, or turned into a flower or a reed or a constellation: how shall we transpose that into a lower key? How shall we imagine what it all might mean if we were to slow down the metamorphosis and follow inch by inch the process of transposition in the one thus chosen as the object of the god's desire? Was it painful for Syrinx to be changed into a reed, no matter how lovely the music ultimately furnished by that reed? What did Daphne feel as she was turning into a laurel?

This approach—of slowing down the metamorphosis and of scrutinizing the unfolding of the process which is only touched upon in the myths themselves by a phrase or so—this would seem to furnish very fruitful possibilities for fiction. And no doubt it might, although the genre would wear thin perhaps after a few fictional reworkings of Ovid, say. But Lewis has carried the process one subtle step further by taking for his protagonist, not Psyche, but this character of his own fabricating, namely Orual. She is the one *left out*. Ah now: how does the whole drama look from that unhappy vantage point?

By doing this, Lewis has brought the drama much closer to us than would have been the case if he had chosen Psyche as his protagonist. For which of us is not Orual? Which of us is not plagued by an ugly face? Who among us feels like Psyche: loved by the gods, pure, beautiful, radiant, sylph-like? Oh dear, no. Oh dear me, no. I'm afraid I'm all warped and twisted and unfortunate, and bedeviled with ungenerous thoughts and turbulent feelings that tend to disclose themselves in all sorts of petty monstrosities like anger and offense and pusillanimity and jealousy and one thing and another. But of course none of this is really my *fault*: if I had had the advantages that she has enjoyed, and if they had only *told* me, and—and we are off and running with Orual's complaint against the gods, which is what Lewis has chosen for his retelling of the Cupid and Psyche myth, with this difference: that in this telling of it, we find the materials carried into the service of the very thing of which the cult of Eros is itself only a dim foreshadowing.

For that cult will tell us of the ecstasy of love, especially physical love; and it will hint, by making the lover a god, at the mystery into which this passionate form of love opens. It will even carry the suggestion that this bliss comes from the gods and will return to the gods. But then what about any connection between this myth and our mortal experience? If we suspect, as we all do, that somehow the myths are of a piece with our experience, then what exactly is the experience which is bespoken in the cult of Eros, especially in the story of Cupid and Psyche? Perhaps it is that we are made for bliss. Perhaps it may be believed that the gods desire us, and will come to us. But I find hints and guesses of this sort of thing only in fugitive reveries, brought on if ever by the sight of a beautiful face or the sound of a Mozart flute concerto or the smell of wild raspberries. If there is anything to it, it has left only its footprint in our experience.

Orual, or we, might tend to adopt some such line as that. It's all very well for the Psyches of this world, but as for the rest of us it's one foot in front of the other, right through to the bitter end.

Oh. The end? What end? Where are you going? On which path are you placing your feet, one in front of the other? Is it going somewhere? Death? Are you sure that is all? How do you know that you may not be *obliged* to come to joy? How do you know that you also will not be—nay, have not been—desired by the god? Indeed—what if you also are Psyche?

This, alas, is what the god says to Orual. In the terrible scene when the tally of Orual's machinations—or say, if we will, with Orual, the tally of her efforts to rescue Psyche from the evil that has befallen her—when that tally is complete, and everything is in ruins, the god turns to Orual.

> *A monster—the Shadowbrute that I and all Glome had imagined—would have subdued me less than the beauty this face wore. And I think anger (what men call anger) would have been more supportable than the passionless and measureless rejection with which it looked upon me. . . . He rejected, denied, answered, and (worst of all) he knew, all I had thought, done or been. . . . He made it to be as if, from the beginning, I had known that Psyche's lover was a god, and as if all my doubtings . . . had been trumped-up foolery, dust blown in my own eyes by myself. You who read my book, judge. Was it so? Or, at least, had it been so in the very past, before this god changed the past? And if they can indeed change the past, why do they never do so in mercy?*[8]

This stands at the end of a long process in which it becomes more and more impossible for us to share Orual's point of view. We find ourselves nudged and crowded along, despite ourselves, to the god's viewpoint, again not because he has slipped some information to us that Orual does not have (he hasn't) but because her own narrative damns her. But then we also find that we do not have the luxury of

[8] Ibid., p. 173.

dissociating ourselves from her. Not one thought that she has, not one scheme, that we don't recognize as all too bleakly familiar.

On her way to the mountain with Bardia after the Great Offering, to rescue Psyche, for example, we find this. She sees herself as the great and noble and selfless heroine, going out into the wilderness to do what she can for the honor and memory of Psyche, even if it is only a matter of picking up and decently burying Psyche's bones. No one else shares this lonely burden. Only the faithful sister, who alone in the world has truly loved Psyche, will do this service. What a heavy day. What a burden of grief. How black the world is.

The difficulty here is that the day turns out to be beautiful, and the landscape irresistibly lovely. Why should Orual's heart not dance? Because (she insists) that would be inappropriate. I am *supposed* to be grief-stricken. That is my role. I must hang on to this bitterness at all costs. I must resist and reject this loveliness. I must not sing. I *will* not sing.

And we cannot get through the scene without hearing the voices of the damned souls in *The Great Divorce* who love their anger and their grief more than they love what they see. If life is bitter for Orual, it may be—alas, it just might be—that it is because she wishes it to be bitter. But what a heavy sentence: to be blameworthy for the very thing that (I tell myself) I have never asked for and cannot (I tell myself) get free from.

An interesting light is thrown on Orual by her juxtaposition here and elsewhere in the action with the faithful retainer and soldier Bardia. He is an utterly true man—transparently brave, simple, and courteous. He is no philosopher, but in him we see the good stock responses that

Lewis lauded in his *Preface to Paradise Lost* and other essays. He will not mix in the quarrel between Trom and Ungit over the Great Offering. "I'm for the King of Glome and the gods of Glome while I live. But if the King and the gods fall out, you great ones must settle it between you. I'll not fight against powers and spirits."[9] He is unfailingly courteous to Orual, seeing real bravery in her and teaching her to use a sword. As he and Orual approach the place on the mountain where Psyche had been left, he is full of the awe and uncertainty that good men feel in the precincts of the ineffable. When Psyche appears, and Orual babbles in wild joy through tears and laughter, feeling no holy fear ("What? I to fear the very Psyche whom I had carried in my arms and taught to speak and to walk?")[10] it is Bardia who recognizes Psyche as the bride of the god—as a goddess even—and wails in terror, throwing earth on his forehead. And, much later, when Orual demands to know what sort of lover this might be who will not allow his bride to see his face, Bardia, after a silence, says, "I should say it was one whose face and form would give her little pleasure if she saw them."[11]

What has taught Bardia all this? He knows no philosophy and very little religion. Is it not that Bardia is "naturally" in tune with the whole mystery, the whole rhythm or dance or pattern, of things, unlike Orual, because he is entirely unaware of and uninterested in himself? His whole life has been the straightforward matter of obedience to custom and rule and decency: obedience to his sovereign, love and faithfulness to his wife, bravery in battle, hard work in his daily tasks, and so forth. That has been his work in life,

[9] Ibid., p. 53.
[10] Ibid., p. 102.
[11] Ibid., p. 136.

cut out for him by his role as soldier, husband, subject. If there are rights that he ought to be demanding, or self-actualization that he ought to be seeking, he has been unaware of it, and it would be difficult in the extreme for us to get him interested in the topic at all. He is a variation on the theme of which Puddleglum is also a variation: utter selflessness; utter unawareness of self at all.

The importance of all this to the drama here is that this selflessness is what is asked by the gods, not by way of tormenting us and denying us our joy, but because that is the pattern of reality; that is the way the Dance is choreographed. Obedience—courtesy—life laid down—joy—liberty—hilarity: that is what it *looks like*, that Dance. Without ever having heard of the Dance, Bardia has long since learned the steps. Orual on the other hand, anxious, frenzied, sullen, embittered, driven, hagridden by the laborious task of justifying her own course of action, punctiliously, ineluctably—she cannot see it. Or will not see it. It is too hateful, this joy. I would rather validate myself and be miserable than give it over and be filled with joy. Better to reign in hell than serve in heaven.

Psyche's path to joy seems simple so far. We see her privileged by the gods to enjoy great beauty and goodness in her own makeup, then go through dramatic but quick suffering, then enter into her joy. Well! If my story could be like that I would be a goddess too. Psyche never had to struggle with paralyzing ambiguity, or with a debility like ugliness, or with divine mockery. Here she is in rosy health, drinking the wine of the gods and enjoying the embraces of her celestial lover, and it all came about so cleanly and quickly. It is not fair.

Every exchange in the conversation between Orual and Psyche here on the mountain painfully dramatizes the chasm between them. Orual sees Psyche as crazed and starving—but then why this blooming health? She tries to plan Psyche's escape, but cannot stop Psyche talking about her palace. And when Psyche tells her story, Orual leaps at every hint that the whole thing might have been an illusion. When Psyche tells of the horrible desolation that assailed her when she was left alone at the tree (and in that scene how can we not hear the echo of "Eloi, Eloi!"), Orual is glad. Perhaps, she thinks, now we can get through to Psyche with the bleak truth. But, oddly, Psyche's tale whispers with echoes of Orual's own story. Psyche's face, for example, was gilded until it did not seem to be her own. Apparently she needed a new face before she was ready to meet the god. We will presently see Orual decide to obliterate her own face altogether and go through life veiled, hiding the ugliness that has been her bane since birth. What is all this about having to have our faces covered and made new before we face the gods?

And Psyche talks as though Orual is only half-awake so far, and that the very telling of Psyche's story will be the thing that will rouse Orual. From Psyche's point of view, becoming able to see the god in his beauty is simply a matter of waking up. Ironically Orual has already bitterly observed the same thing, but from the underside: "Now mark yet again the cruelty of the gods. There is no escape from them into sleep or madness, for they can pursue you into them with dreams. Indeed you are then most at their mercy. The nearest thing we have to a defence against them (but there is no real defence) is to be very wide awake and sober and hard at work, to hear no music, never to look at earth or sky, and (above all) to love no one." [12] From Orual's point of view, staying awake is a matter of being on guard;

[12] Ibid., pp. 80–81.

from Psyche's it is a matter of being able to taste and see joy. From Orual's point of view Psyche's experience of bliss is a drugged illusion from which she must be wakened. From Psyche's, Orual's experience of bitterness is a drugged illusion from which *she* must be wakened.

But this is to leap ahead too fast. Orual has hardly begun to understand. Psyche's recitation of what has happened, which could be arrayed point for point on one side of a ledger and found to correspond exactly, point for point, with the paradoxical language of the saints—it all is nonsense to Orual. Worse, it is sacrilege. Psyche, in her passion, knew that there was a connection between this ritual and the return of rain and health to Glome—something the old priest knew, but not the Fox. Nonsense. Psyche saw the Westwind. *Him*, not *it*. Nonsense. Psyche felt leprous and ashamed—not of her sin, or her naked femininity, but of her mortality: something she couldn't help. Nonsense. Psyche saw that everything that had happened in her life before her passion had been the dream, and that this was waking reality. Nonsense. She found herself now in the house not merely where the god was worshipped, but where he lived. Nonsense again. He called it *her house*. She was given wine and fruit by unseen hands. Rubbish and illusion and tragedy.

And Orual: "Psyche . . . I can't bear this any longer. . . . If this is all true, I've been wrong all my life. Everything has to be begun over again." [13]

Her worst fear—and the cold truth.

"My whole heart leaped to shut the door against something monstrously amiss . . . infinite misgiving—the whole world (Psyche with it) slipping out of my hands . . . something hateful. . . . I was as weak beside her as the Fox beside

[13] Ibid., p. 115.

the Priest. . . . For the world had broken in pieces and Psyche and I were not on the same piece."[14] She is being unmade.

Orual's reactions are too transparent. This god? "What have I to do with him?", her very words once again answering verbatim the evil spirits who saw the god in another Story. This god? "Where is this god? Where is he? Show him to me!" No, Orual: it can't be done on a dare. "We'll cure you." Do I look as though I have been eating only berries? "I don't want it! I hate it. Hate it, hate it, hate it." Alas, child. "Come back to me, Psyche." No, Maia: you must come to me.

"I learned then how one can hate those one loves." The destruction wrought in the soul by its insistence on its own illusions has nearly reached the nadir. The reverse transubstantiation by which love becomes hate has occurred. It needs only to be sealed and perfected by the conscious, calculated, prolonged, and willed refusal of sheer fact. Orual sees the palace, and knows it. But, since this undeniable reality will not fit the story she is fabricating—and there can no longer be much pretense that her telling of it is true, or that she wishes it to be true—then she will suppress the fact, both in her mind and in her reports to Bardia. She dares to challenge us, the readers, with "you who read, give judgment. . . . What is the use of a sign which is itself only another riddle?"[15] This mesh of mendacity thickens with time: later we find Orual allowing Psyche to misinterpret something she has said, telling herself, "But if that was what she took out of my words, I thought it no part of my duty to set her right. It was an error helping her towards the main truth. I had need of all help to drive her thither."[16] Yes; just as Weston must destroy the universe in order to

[14] Ibid., pp. 117–20.
[15] Ibid., p. 133.
[16] Ibid., p. 161.

bring about his Utopia, or Belbury must bulldoze the countryside and torture people in order to usher in its spectacular paradise, or Stalin must kill one hundred million people in order to inaugurate the dictatorship of the proletariat. How do those horrors start?

There is a provocative development presently in the conversations between Orual and the Fox about these mysteries. By this time Orual is all too aware of what the truth of the matter is turning out to be, namely what Bardia or the Priest would assume it is. But the Fox, in the watery light of reason, has useful and consoling explanations for everything. Everything can be explained according to "Nature", without reaching for the frantic alternative of supposing that anything *divine* is happening. But then we come upon a hint that perhaps even the view of Bardia and the Priest is not altogether adequate: their supposition as faithful followers of the cult of Ungit has been that of course Psyche has been devoured or otherwise sacrificed. Ironically, the only one among them who remotely suspects the real truth of the matter is Orual, and that for entirely the wrong reasons. She alone has entertained the fleeting thought, or hope, that the Brute might in fact be the heavenly lover that Psyche speaks of; that what appears dark and chaotic and cruel from the underside (the best that the earthy and bloody cult of Ungit can do), or else simply passionless and impersonal (the best that the Fox can do), might turn out to both hide and hint at joys beyond anyone's ability to hope for. But Orual must discount this last possibility for two reasons: it does not fit her case against the gods; and it is clearly attributable to weak and wishful thinking. (We find at the end, of course, that both the Fox and Bardia are "saved", because each has obeyed with constancy and courage as much of the truth as he did see.)

In all of this the reader is forced into the uncomfortable position of so deeply understanding and hence sympathizing with Orual's position that he could almost find it in himself to welcome events that would vindicate her. Or put it another way: the vantage point to which the reader is crowded forces him to make room in his imagination for a story in which all that is cruel and chaotic, far from being reversed at the last moment (thus snatching the whole tale from the jaws of tragedy), turns out to be the very agent of joy—nay more, turns out to be, by some divine alchemy too strong for us to bear at the moment, the underside of joy itself. It never was anything other than joy.

Everyone is wrong and right at the same time. Orual is wrong in her grim program of self-vindication with its corollary of hatred to the gods, but right in what she has glimpsed (and wishes she hadn't); the Fox is wrong in failing to see that reasonable maxims will not account for everything, but right in almost everything he says about how we should behave, and also, ironically, in his supposition that things must be according to Nature (they must, but Nature is far deeper and more mysterious than he is aware of); and the cult of Ungit is wrong in having no real promise of light and joy, and in trapping everyone into a ceaseless and hopeless treadmill of fear and propitiation, but right in knowing that blood and ritual and taboo are the paths to the very frontier of Reality.

It is always difficult to track down the exact turning point in a drama. But my own inclination would be to see it in the crashing, apocalyptic scene at the end of Orual's second visit to the mountain. There everything is brought to a head, and falls to ruins, and there begins the long, grim trek for both Psyche and Orual. But at least for Orual it is a trek which, like Dante's, without ever appearing to change directions, turns out in retrospect to have been "up". Just as Dante, when he reached the bottom of hell at the center of the world then began the path up toward Mount Purgatory and Paradise without ever perceiving a turn in the path, so Orual now goes back to Glome and years of sadness and flatness and bearing of responsibility that turn out to be purgatorial and hence sanctifying. (We find this out in an epilogue: Orual's story ends just as she stumbles up to the threshold of joy.)

The climactic scene there on the mountain, when Orual's schemes achieve their desired end of "rescuing" Psyche from the god, brings all the dramatic currents to a head. Orual presses her case against the gods to its implacably logical conclusion: "*Show* me. Make him show *you*. If he is what he says he is. . . . " We cannot escape hearing the echo, like an antiphon from another Story, "If thou beest the son of God. . . ." Psyche cannot answer Orual, not because there is no answer, but because Orual's ears have no way of beginning to hear it. It would be sacrilege to cast these pearls before those swinish ears. All of the motions and energies of Orual's "love" for Psyche come to a point in her supernally tyrannous act of self-immolation when she stabs herself in order to "save" Psyche. It is the black mass: the very words and gestures of love, warped into the service of hatred and self-will. And Psyche capitulates: "This is the price you have put upon your life. Well, I must pay it." [17] How true this is neither she nor Orual can dream of yet: Psyche goes out weeping into exile to pay the price of Orual's sin; but, in the strange paradoxes so dear to the gods, Orual goes into *her* exile now, to bear (it turns out) the burden of Psyche's sorrow.

[17] Ibid., p. 166.

The first thing Orual decides upon her return to Glome is that she will go veiled from now on. She will have, for all intents and purposes, no face. She sees it as "a treaty made with my ugliness". The gods (and we, by this time) may see it as perhaps the first gesture made, albeit unwittingly, in the direction of truth. For the truth is that she has no face, if by face we mean an identity that may look upon the gods and may receive their gaze. Then she settles upon a program of extinguishing all vulnerability and joy from herself—of sealing up everything, as it were: the past, her feelings, her womanhood. She will be busy. She takes up the weight of queenship, for old Trom is dying. In time both he and the old priest die, and she is queen indeed. Not only this, but she becomes the champion of Glome in single-sword combat with Argan of Phars, to save the head of the good Trunia. The doubts and terrors that assail her before this combat, undertaken for Glome and for Trunia and quite without reference to any program she might ever have had of vindicating herself against the gods, set up echoes in our imagination of the Wilderness and Gethsemane in another Story of a champion going alone into battle for others' sake.

And all the while she is haunted by the sound of something or someone weeping. It may be the chain in a well in the palace courtyard. But it sounds like Psyche, or somebody. Also, something inside of Orual seems to be shriveling and dying, like a reverse pregnancy. It becomes less and less clear as one listens to her tale whether this weeping is to be construed as the mere squeak of a chain, or Psyche in her exile, or perhaps the thing dying in Orual. Or rather, it becomes more and more clear that it is all three, or that it does not matter which it is.

She becomes completely preoccupied. Being queen, and bearing the entire burden of Glome—wars, domestic justice, crops, everything—leaves her no room for anything else. It is as though there are two personages now: the receding Orual and the emerging queen. She sustains the traumas, bitter to Orual but necessary for a queen, of realizing that her retainers are precisely that—retainers, not possessions. The Fox must be set free, and even though he chooses to stay, her momentary glimpse of his reverie about the beauty of his native land makes it clear to her that there are things dearer to him than anything she can offer. He is not hers. That must die, Orual. And Bardia: this wife of his, always a small vexation to Orual, bears a child, and it is a jolt to Orual to realize that he has a life other than his duties in the palace. She had always assumed that he was hers and hers alone. That too must die, Orual. The scene in which Orual finds out (from his wife Ansit) the true story of Bardia, after his death, reveals with terrible clarity one more variation on the theme of Orual's devouring tyranny over every object that she thought she loved. Loving and devouring come to the same thing with her, in a ghastly parody of the blissful mystery hinted at in Psyche's immolation and nuptials, in which the loving and the devouring seem to be the same thing (is she the god's bride, or his victim?).

Various developments in Glome seem to accompany the queen's reign. After the death of the old priest, the religion of Ungit seems somehow weakened. The new, young priest, Arnom, cleans out the sanctuary, lightens things up, and sets up the image of a beautiful woman which had been made, not in Glome or even Greece, but in some land that had learned of Greece (could it be Rome?). The Fox grows old and dies, talking more and more of poetry and less and less of philosophy as he nears death. He also mistakes Orual for Psyche frequently now: clearly his eyesight is getting sharper.

Once on a royal progress through the neighboring kingdom of Essur the queen pauses at the shrine of what turns
out to be a very recently godded goddess. The attendant
priest, in response to the queen's question, tells her the story
of this goddess whose name is Istra (which had been Psyche's
other name, it will be recalled). Orual's agitation grows fiercer
and fiercer as he meanders on and on through the tale, the
trouble being that he has got it all *wrong*. In this version,
Istra's wicked sisters both visit her, and, seeing her palace
clearly, destroy it through jealousy. Oh, the cynicism of the
gods—to let this version of things get abroad! Then it turns
out the poor priest has got the tale all mixed in with the
yearly vegetation rites of this shrine. "He knew nothing.
The story and the worship were all one in his mind." [18] It
has not occurred to Orual yet that if a story is true we may
see it cropping up under various guises—in cult, in old lore,
and in the very cycles of earth itself, with seedtime and
harvest answering to the rituals and the tales. How do seeds
live again? Is there any resurrecting of the things that we in
our cruelty have slain? Any life from death anywhere?

Orual returns home and writes out her case. The gods
have been unfair. They are noxious. My case is unanswer-
able. Here is the end of my book ...

... except that the act of writing it all down has dis-
lodged something. "Memory, once waked, will play the
tyrant." [19] The gods "used my own pen to probe my
wound." [20] Memories begin to drift back to her. Her bitch
sister Redival: what about her? Perhaps she had some feelings after all. And Bardia: have I killed him? The labor of
sifting through the past with its jumble of motives spills

[18] Ibid., p. 246.
[19] Ibid., p. 253.
[20] Ibid., p. 254.

into Orual's sleep, with laborious dreams of sifting through huge piles of mixed seeds, trying to sort them into piles.

Then Orual must sit, as queen, with Arnom the priest, in the temple of Ungit, as part of the Year's birth. Does the rite have any real efficacy? Is there any connection between the Year's birth and Arnom's sham and ritual fight to get out of the temple? And who, really, is Ungit here, this humped, faceless shape? Why does the old peasant woman prefer to make sacrifice to the old dreadful Ungit rather than to the lovelier new statue? Arnom has some vaguely Greek and vaguely plausible explanations for things, but it leaves Orual with the uneasy sense that perhaps all the tidying up and fumigating of the rite which he has attempted does not come as close in on the central mysteries as the blood and incense and darkness of the old cult.

The things that are happening to Orual now seem to constitute a systematic "replay" of her whole life. First, in her labor of sifting the seeds of her past, came Redival: "I had never thought how it might be with her".[21] Then Bardia: have I devoured him too? Now, when she returns home from the temple rite it is her father who appears to her in a dream. At his hest she must go, it seems, to the Pillar Room where all the business of the kingdom has always been carried on, and she must break through the floor and throw herself into what seems to be a well. Down and down she must go, through layer after layer, farther into earth and rock, "below any dens that foxes can dig", says her father. No Greek can come at this deep level of things. Finally, when there is no room to dodge anything and she is hemmed in by living rock, the king asks her, "Who is Ungit?" and taking her to a mirror, bids her look in. The face that looks

[21] Ibid., p. 256.

back at her is the face of Ungit. "I am Ungit", she wails. And with that she is back out in the daylight.

Her "confession" of this terrible thing has released her from at least that ordeal. "It was I who was Ungit. That ruinous face was mine. I was that ... all-devouring, womb-like, yet barren, thing ... gorged with men's stolen lives." [22]

She will attempt not to be Ungit—by suicide (useless) or by stoic resolve toward self-improvement (also useless). Ah: she will try a new disguise. Since all men know her now by her veil, she will go unveiled. She will show her face: "For I thought I would look as like Ungit to them as I had seen myself to be in that mirror beneath the earth. As like Ungit? I *was* Ungit: I in her and she in me." [23]

Lewis has not blundered unwittingly from this heathen tale into the language of Saint John 17 here. It must be that in *all* tales there is a union of the gods with us mortals. How that may be, or what exactly happens in the "in-godding", no one can say: Lewis, being Christian, knew that some such mystery lies at the root of things.

The sense in which the visionary sequence of ordeals in which we find Orual caught up now, and which we cannot avoid recognizing as quite clearly purgatorial—the sense in which this involves a "replay" of everything she has ever done or said or felt, is intimated in the king's comment to her as they dig. Work, he insists. "Do you mean to slug abed all your life?" And we are straight back at Orual's testy comment about Bardia in his last sickness: does he mean to slug abed for the rest of his life? Apparently the measure with which Orual meted is being meted out to her now.

[22] Ibid., p. 276.
[23] Ibid., p. 278.

But the visionary set of exchanges, so to call them, in which we now see Orual encountering and tasting all her past attitudes and misdeeds, far from being merely retributive or retaliatory on the part of the gods, turns out to be matched, point for point, with exchanges by which Orual is *helped* along this difficult track of purgation. She is hindered, for example, in an attempt to drown herself by tying her own ankles and leaping into the river in despair, by a voice crying, "Do not do it." She knows it to be the voice of a god: "Who should know better than I? A god's voice had once shattered my whole life. They are not to be mistaken." [24] Somewhere in here the whole case, that the gods will not speak to us in any recognizable way, seems to have drained away completely.

And now the process speeds to the final unfolding. Orual, as did Psyche in Apuleius' tale, tries to gather the golden fleece of the divine rams, but is trampled by the rams, not in their anger but in their joy. She is unable, in this vision, to bear the sheer force of the Divine Beauty. She sees another woman gathering the fleece quite unperturbed: "She won without effort what utmost effort would not win for me." [25] Ah, comfortless: well, at least I have one rag to hold on to. My love for Psyche was blameless.

Was it? Now another vision for Orual. She must fill a bowl with the water of death and give it to Ungit (Ungit must die, clearly). Impossible. But somehow the bowl has become in her hand her book of complaints, the way things will do in dreams, and she must read out to the assembled tribunal (Trom, the Fox, and thousands of others) her case. But the book has shriveled—"a little, shabby, crumpled thing,

[24] Ibid., p. 279.
[25] Ibid., p. 284.

nothing like my great book that I had worked on all day, day after day.... It was all a vile scribble; each stroke mean and yet savage, like the snarl of my father's voice...."[26] (Ah: like Trom, are you? The motes you saw in his eye—motes of ill temper and pusillanimity—mere motes to your beam perhaps?) Well, read your case.

Somehow the case comes out that the gods' fault is that they are too beautiful and that they lure away from us those whom we love. "We'd rather you drank their blood than stole their hearts. We'd rather they were ours and dead than yours and made immortal."[27] Oh, Orual—now we are getting in toward the truth. And what's this? You *did* have enough signs that her palace was real? You *could* have known the truth if you had wanted? Then what?

> *But how could I want to know it? Tell me that? The girl was mine. What right had you to steal her away? ... That there should be gods at all, there's our misery and bitter wrong. There's no room for you and us in the same world.... We want to be our own. I was my own and Psyche was mine, and no one else has any right to her.... What should I care for some horrible, new happiness which I hadn't given her and which separated her from me? ... She was mine. Mine: do you not know what the word means? Mine!*[28]

But it seems that Orual has been reading this over and over and over to the assembled company. Now the judge: "Are you answered?" "Yes."

For: "The complaint was the answer.... I saw why the gods do not speak to us openly, nor let us answer. Till that

[26] Ibid., pp. 289–90.
[27] Ibid., p. 291.
[28] Ibid., pp. 291, 292.

word can be dug out of us, why should they hear the bab-
ble that we think we mean? How can they meet us face to
face till we have faces?" [29]

And now the Fox, like Virgil for Dante, must be Orual's
guide, to take her to the final mysteries. But this is the Fox
redeemed—the Fox who himself now has learned that "there
must be sacrifices"; the Fox, penitent, who asks the judge
to send him away to Tartarus (hell) "if Tartarus can cure
glibness. I made her think that a prattle of maxims would
do, all thin and clear as water." [30]

Apparently all here is guilt—guilt revealed, owned, expi-
ated, and forgiven. It is the Fox, her old tutor, who now
brings Orual to the final panorama where she is given to
see the other side of what she has been experiencing.

It is a fresco with a series of stories painted on a wall.
They are the incidents through which Orual has just come—
the suicide attempt at the river, the piles of seeds, the golden
wool, and the bowl/book—with this oddity, that in each
case it is Psyche who is the subject of the painting. Orual
asks the Fox if it is all true. Yes. Then how can Psyche have
come through? "Another bore all the anguish." [31]

But there is one more ordeal for Psyche: she must go
to the deadlands and get the casket full of beauty for Ungit,
so that Ungit will be transformed (Nature herself, red in
tooth and claw, must be redeemed and glorified before
the story is over). She must speak to no one on her way,
and it is a dread irony that the two tempters who might
cause her to waver here are shades of the Fox and of
Orual—an Orual whose arm drips with blood and who
wails, "Oh Psyche.... Oh, my own child, my only love....

[29] Ibid., p. 294.
[30] Ibid., p. 295.
[31] Ibid., p. 300.

Come back to Maia." [32] But Psyche presses on, suffering a pain greater than that of the pleading Orual.

On her return with the casket, it is Psyche who raises the prone Orual to her feet. The picture now is like the pictures that we find at the end of *The Last Battle, Perelandra,* and *That Hideous Strength,* and also some of the glimpses in *The Great Divorce.* Lewis is talking about regions that defy art. Dante, Milton, Hopkins, and Eliot, at least, have struggled with this, to say nothing of Saint John the Divine. How do you speak—under what species will you speak—of the Beatific Vision? How will you catch the tail of glory? The Ineffable is, precisely, ineffable.

Take Psyche, for example: her beauty is the beauty of a goddess.

> *And yet (this is hard to say) with all this, even because of all this, she was the old Psyche still; a thousand times more her very self than she had been before the Offering. For all that had then but flashed out in a glance or a gesture, all that one meant most when one spoke her name, was now wholly present. . . . Goddess? I had never seen a real woman before.* [33]

Here we glimpse in a myth what Lewis tried to come at in his essays "Transposition" and "The Weight of Glory".

But this is all nothing. As mere torches pale when the sunlight floods in, so everything grows pale with the advent of the god himself now. He comes, alas, to judge Orual. "If Psyche had not held me by the hand I should have sunk down." [34] Even the Fox cannot help her here. The one

[32] Ibid., p. 304.
[33] Ibid., p. 306.
[34] Ibid., p. 307.

who bears her now must be one who has already been this way. "The air was growing brighter and brighter. . . . Each breath I drew let into me new terror, joy, overpowering sweetness. I was pierced through and through with the arrows of it." [35] Again, the very phraseology cannot be a mistake: the Mother of God in another Story was pierced with arrows that appeared to be arrows of sorrow at first, but the flesh that bore this pain bore, by this pain, God. The bringing of glory to birth from Nature is a painful business. "I was being unmade. I was no one." [36] ("Be it unto me according to thy word", said the woman in another Story.)

The paradoxes pile up. There is no way other than narrative to say the thing.

> But that's little to say; rather Psyche herself was, in a manner, no one. I loved her as I would once have thought it impossible to love; would have died any death for her. And yet, it was not, not now, she that really counted. Or if she counted (and oh, gloriously she did) it was for another's sake. The earth and stars and sun, all that was or will be, existed for his sake. And he was coming. The most dreadful, the most beautiful, the only dread and beauty there is, was coming. [37]

And then the voice of the god: "You also are Psyche". [38] And, as Orual's first book ended with the assurance that the gods do not speak because they have no answer, so this one ends with the acknowledgment that, indeed, they do not speak (as it were), because *they themselves are the answer.*

[35] Ibid.
[36] Ibid.
[37] Ibid.
[38] Ibid., p. 308.

Or rather, by now it is "You Yourself are the answer." [39]
She has seen him. "Before your face questions die away.
What other answer would suffice?" [40]

It is left to Arnom, the new priest, to append a brief
note. Orual has died, after her vision. She was, he says,
"The most wise, just, valiant, fortunate, and merciful of all
the princes known in our parts of the world." [41]

Who? Orual? Wise? Just? Valiant? Merciful? From whence
did those virtues arise? The only Orual we have met was
foolish, cruel, mendacious, tyrannical. Indeed, yes. That is
why she had to die, had to shrivel away weeping, and die;
while the Queen of Glome, imposed upon this Orual from
the outside by duties and heavy responsibilities, with never
a moment to think of herself, had to grow. Every just judgment handed down for the people of Glome, every battle
fought, every slave freed, every duty carried out, was somehow accounted as "answering to" all the clutter of pettiness
and cruelty and perfidy accrued by the old Orual.

The process by which the gods transfigure nature—
Orual's dark, bloody, self-serving nature, which may be called
Ungit—*and* Ungit herself, red in tooth and claw everywhere we look, and demanding sacrifice and holocaust—
the process is long and painful—as long and painful as a
gestation and birth; and the fruit of the pain is bliss. The
child's name, in Apuleius' old story, was Volupta: Pleasure.
From the union of the god with our souls comes that fruit.

[39] Ibid.
[40] Ibid.
[41] Ibid., pp. 308–9.